Modern Diesels in Focus

Modern Diesels in Focus

B.J.Nicolle

LONDON

IAN ALLAN LTD

First published 1979

ISBN 0 7110 0981 3

© Ian Allan Ltd 1979

Published by Ian Allan Ltd, Shepperton, Surrey;
and printed in the United Kingdom by
Ian Allan Printing Ltd

Contents

All photographs, unless credited otherwise, are by the author.

Introduction

It has long been a source of frustration to me that so many fire and water enthusiasts declare that there is no comparison between their sparkling steam idols and the modern diesels currently operating on British Railways. Their usual cry is that there is no majesty in a filthy diesel, although to me the sight of an ex-works 'Deltic' at Kings Cross, or a Class 40, fresh out of the works at Crewe diesel depot, can be described as nothing short of awesome. As for the allegation that once you've seen one diesel you have seen them all, I hope that through this volume I shall prove that such a flippant statement cannot be linked to the varied and fascinating range of modern BR traction.

For several years it has been my intention to compile a Diesel volume. With *Modern Diesels in Focus*, I have been able to bring together my work and that of several of my colleagues, all extremely high class photographers, to produce what I consider to be a well-balanced album containing a selection of prints depicting modern main line engines. The photographs in this volume include locomotives, stationary, under construction or repair, as well as in action, from all over the British Railways network. All classes of main line locomotives which attained renumbered status are depicted in this volume. I also include the 'Western' Class 52s as they ran for just over three years alongside their computerised counterparts.

If through *Modern Diesels in Focus*, I bring pleasure to all ardent diesel enthusiasts I shall be well pleased with the efforts of my colleagues and myself, but if I also manage to convert one steam enthusiast to a liking for diesels I shall feel the job has been well done.

Although diesels first appeared on British main lines back in 1955 it was not until 1968 that they finally gained pre-eminence with the withdrawal of the last remaining pockets of steam. Some of the initial classes have now started diminishing, particularly the 24s and 44s which only amount to two and three respectively, although the former once totalled 150. Inroads have also begun to be made into the Classes 20 and 40. These withdrawals, together with the Western Region's hydraulic locomotives are chiefly due to the introduction of Inter-City 125 HSTs, the electrification of the Crewe-Glasgow main line, and the arrival of the Class 56s on the Eastern and London Midland Regions.

Problems with the bogies of early Class 56s initially made their availability rather low, although all of the Romanian-built specimens allocated to Tinsley on the Eastern Region, have now undergone bogie modifications in either Doncaster or Stratford Works. The first 12 Doncaster built locomotives were fitted with the same bogies as the Romanian diesels, and therefore required modification too. No 56.043, delivered to Toton in March 1978, was the first of the class to be fitted with the new style bogies developed by British Rail Engineering Ltd at Derby. At present Doncaster has a further order for 30 more locomotives to be allocated eventually to the Birmingham and Stoke divisions, extensively for use on merry-go-round workings. Although a total of 90 Class 56s has been authorised, the final number of locomotives is likely to be well in excess of this figure as the class is destined to replace Brush Type 4s on almost all MGR. work, whilst the displaced locos will be transferred no doubt, to allow the complete withdrawal of the classes mentioned earlier.

Introduction of the electrified services on the Great Northern suburban routes out of Kings Cross and Moorgate to Royston at the beginning of 1978, allowed the release of electric heat Class 31s to the Western Region for use on the Bristol-Portsmouth run, (previously worked unsatisfactorily by demus).

The once fairly rigid subdivisions in the various classes are gradually being eroded, (particularly in respect of the Classes 45 and 47), in the sense that as more and more of the steam heated Mk 1 passenger stock is being withdrawn from service, except for football specials, reliefs and other excursions, the requirement for boiler-fitted locomotives is obviously diminishing. Consequently, because a Class 47 happens to fall into the 47/0 subdivision series from No 47.001 to No 47.298, it no longer follows that the locomotive retains an operative steam generator. At present 32 members of the subdivision have had their boilers completely removed and replaced by concrete blocks, (for weighting purposes), whilst a further 29 have had the equipment isolated (these totals are always liable to alteration). Even when all coaching stock becomes electrically heated, there will still be a requirement for boiler-fitted locomotives at certain depots to operate steam lances during winter months to free frozen points etc unless another form of de-icer is devised in the near future.

For a number of years it had been British Rail policy not to name any further locomotives; in fact the trend was more to remove the nameplates before vandals did. Classes which have lost their nameplates are of course, the LMR 40s, named after ships, and more recently certain Western Region Class 47s. The Class 50 English Electric locomotives have been recently named and in true Western Region tradition (where they have all been allocated for several years), now carry warship nameplates, many of which were once carried by the Class 42 and 43 hydraulics.

Finally I should like to thank all the photographers whose work appears in this volume and also my wife, without whose help and encouragement this book may never have become a reality.

August 1978   *B. J. Nicolle*

Class 20

Left: A study of a Class 20 No 20.164 taken almost 'nose on' to show the unique profile of the class, the only remaining type of single cabbed main line locomotives currently running on British Railways. No 20.164 is one of no more than a dozen out of a class once totalling 228, still running in green livery, although the yellow warning panels have somewhat altered in recent years.

Below: The Derby stabling point has always been a refuge for Toton based locomotives, particularly on Sundays, and the Class 20s are no exception. Nos 20.164/193/037 and 005 were amongst seven of the class present on 18 June 1978. The pair stabled on the outside of the curve had worked the Derby-Skegness passenger service the day before.

Right: Although only a stabling point for Toton, it is not unusual to see large numbers of the parent depots allocation of Class 20s at Westhouses, particularly at weekends. No 20.158 in green livery and No 20.197 are here seen in multiple, coupled in the usual manner nose to nose, enabling them to be driven from either end like most other types of locomotive.

Below right: No 20.177 has run most of its career in green livery, but has recently come out of Glasgow St Rollox Works after a general overhaul and blue repaint. It is seen here still in green livery in what used to be the depot buildings at Westhouses (until the roof was removed to save on maintenance) with its sister engine No 20.148 and Class 47 No 47.201, the latter now allocated to Cricklewood.

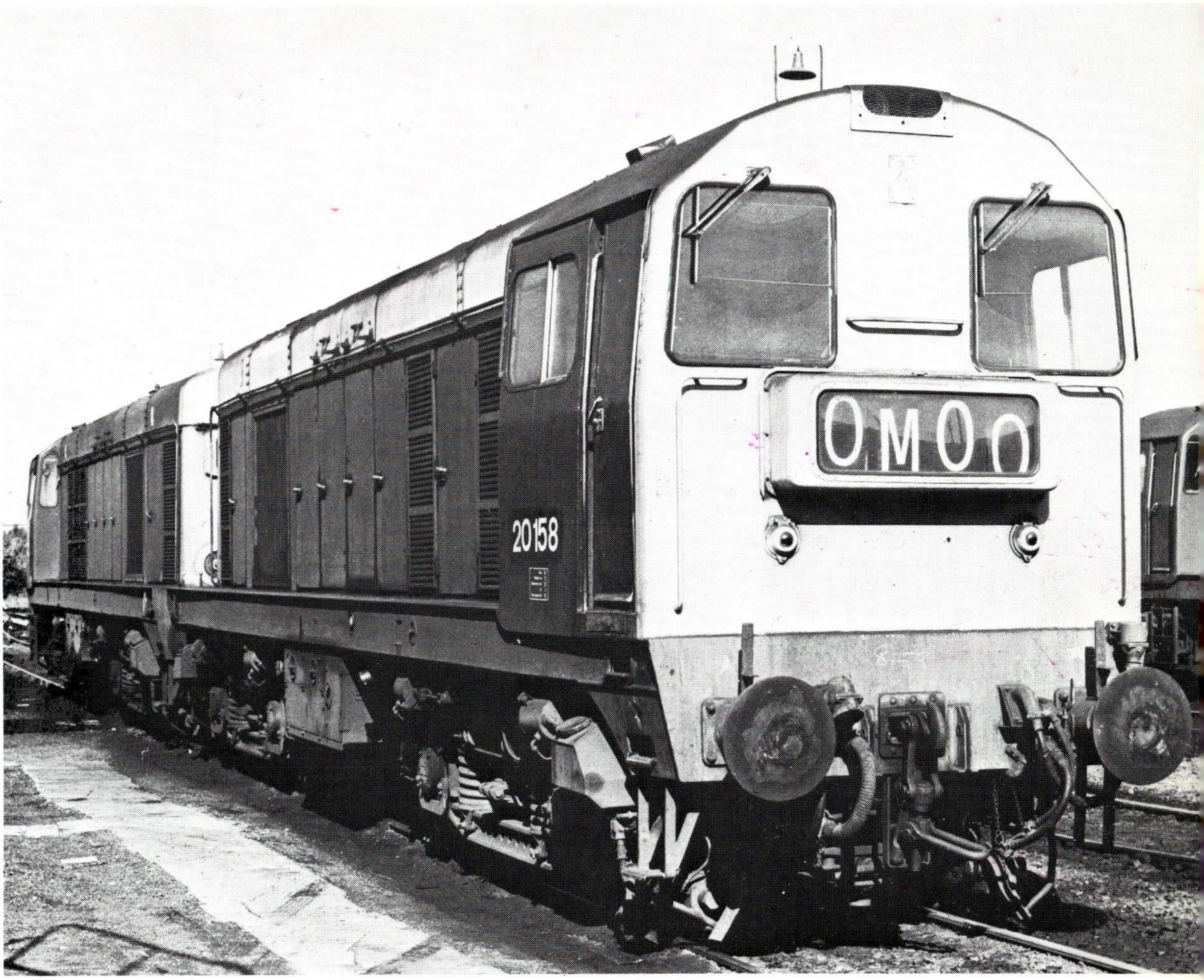

0M00
20158

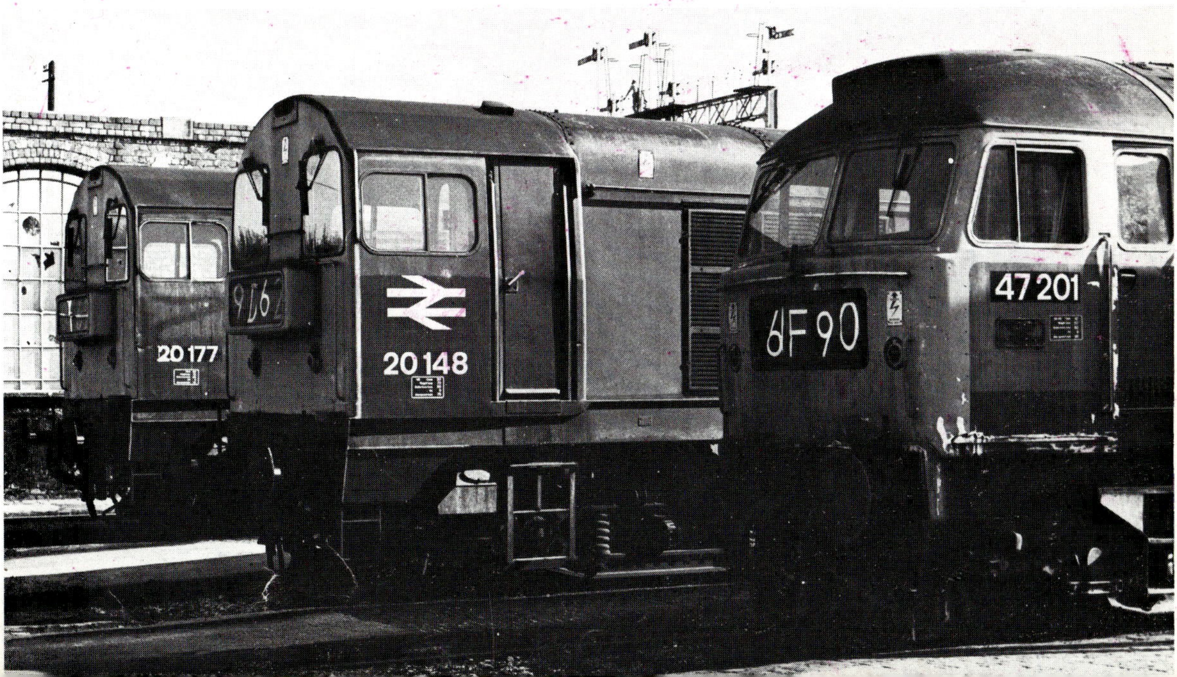

20177
20148
6F90
47201

Left: Eastfield based Class 20s are regular visitors to the Grangemouth, Motherwell and Ayr areas of the Scottish Region. Here, Nos 20.108/121 and 106 pose with No 25.011 on Ayr diesel depot, whilst Nos 20.123 and 20.015, both dual braked, pass with a train of unfitted empty mineral wagons destined for Pennylenie Colliery on 20 April 1976.

Below left: As an exception to the rule Nos 20.168 and 20.199, both allocated to Toton and vacuum braked, pass through Gloucester coupled in multiple in a nose to tail fashion. The locomotives are working the 11.05 8V63 Tinsley to Severn Tunnel Junction freight on 18 August 1976. Although fairly rare in South Wales, Gloucester drivers occasionally take the class as far as Severn Tunnel Junction on such freight turns returning light or with a northbound freight, almost immediately.

Right: A pair of the older disc head-coded Class 20s Nos 20.008 and 20.047, trundle through Churchdown on the outskrits of Cheltenham with the 8V77 11.35 SX Toton to Severn Tunnel Junction mixed freight on 11 July 1977. Although never fitted with any form of carriage heating equipment, earlier members of the class were fitted with steam pipes to enable their use in multiple with other boiler-fitted locomotives. The steam pipes have been removed from No 20.008, but the covered pipe can be clearly seen to the bottom right of the drawbar and coupling.

Below: A striking study in light and dark taken on 29 March 1975 depicts Nos 20.179 and 20.125 resting between turns in the now demolished Polmaldie depot. The locomotive to the left, having its batteries recharged, is fitted with miniature snowploughs and the modern style blind headcodes, whilst the other fitted with disc headcodes shows clearly the snowplough brackets to both the left and right of the drawbar. The token pick-up indentation is also clearly visible below the number of the locomotive on the right.

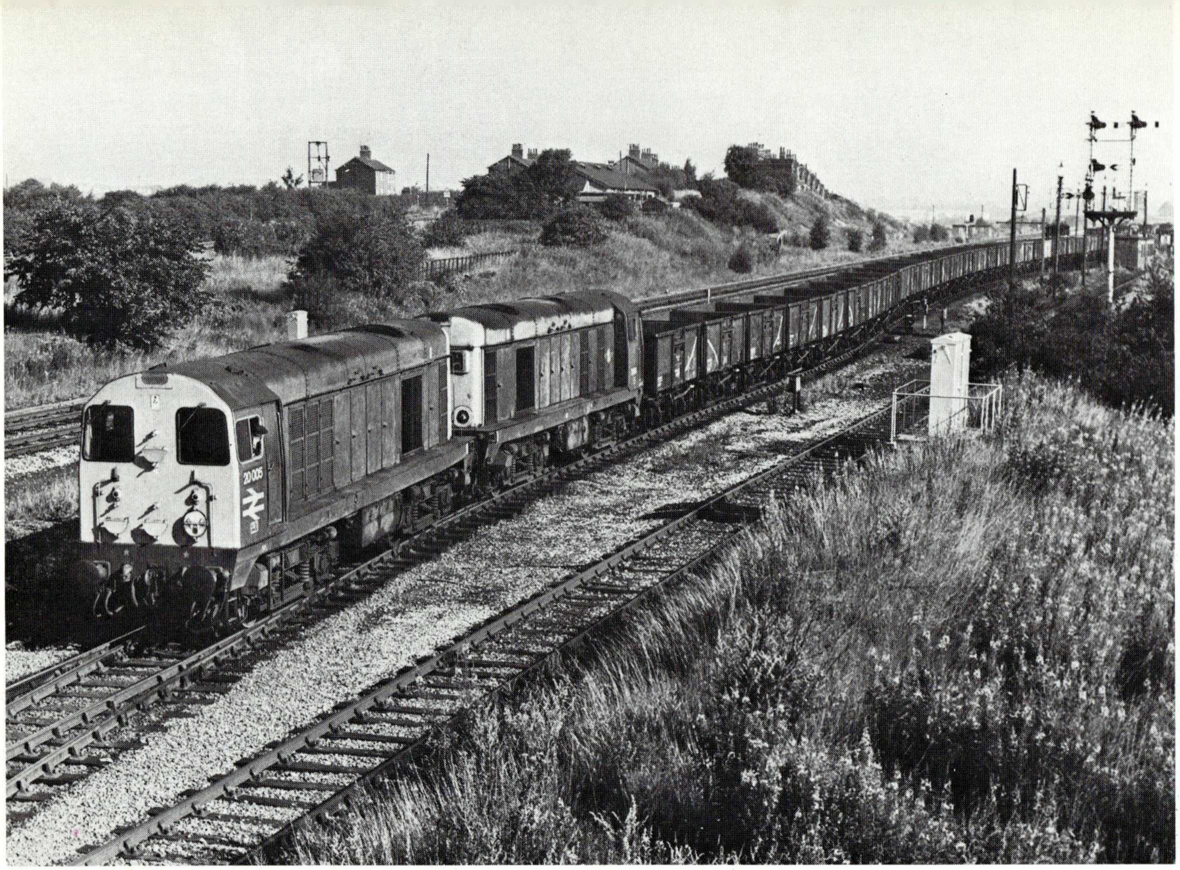

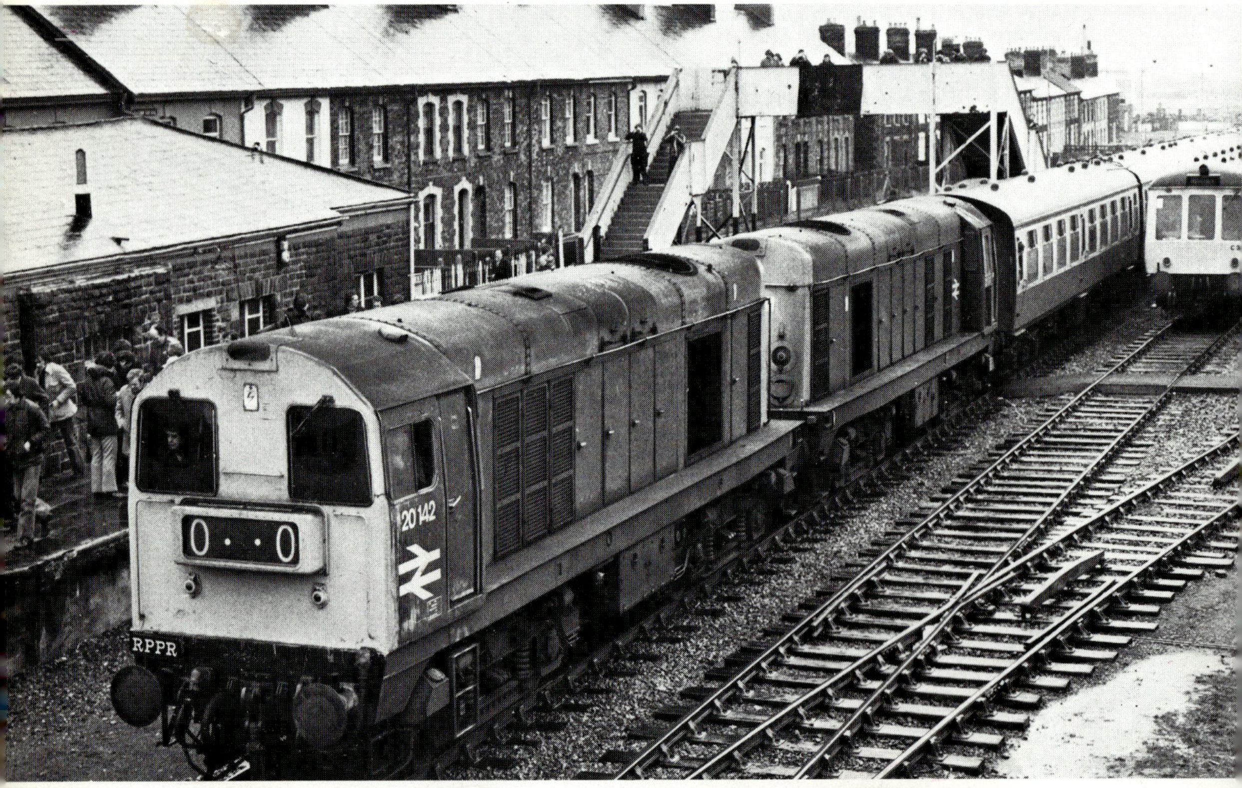
0--0
20 142
RPPR

Top left: Nos 20.005 and 20.163 (in green livery) propel a train of empty mineral wagons into Westhouses up reception sidings on Sunday 18 August 1974, ready no doubt, to be reloaded during the following week.

Left: Although, as already stated, Class 20s are particularly rare on passenger services during the winter months, trends in recent years have been for enthusiasts specials to be either hauled by boilerless freight engines or by passenger locos on unfamiliar regions. Here Nos 20.142 and 20.030 are seen standing at Treherbert in South Wales on the wet wintery afternoon of 29 January 1978 with the 'Deltic Dragon' 08.25 special from Paddington. Class 55 No 55.018, *Ballymoss*, worked the train to and from Cardiff. / *G. R. Hounsell*

Above: During the transitional period from the original numbering system to the computerised one, it was obviously not uncommon to see locomotives running about with either style displayed. The 8M80 12.05(SX) conditional coal freight from Mansfield CS to Toton up sidings seen passing through Sandiacre on 10 April 1974 is in the very capable hands of Tinsley based specimens Nos 20.228 in green livery and 8059, the latter still requiring renumbering.

Right: Shortly before the introduction of computerised renumbering No 8166 is prepared for load bank testing having undergone a general overhaul in Derby Works. The maintenance of the LMR engines has moved from Crewe to Derby and back again in recent years. The Scottish Region has always maintained its own locomotives and is now responsible for the Eastern based ones plus odd LMR engines too.

Class 24

24 124

Class 24/1	
Weight tons	74
Brake force tons	38
ETH index	
RA	5
Max speed mph	75

Haymarket
HA

Right: Specification panel and depot allocation sticker etc in close up of Class 24/1 No 24.124 at Haymarket. This was the last Scottish strong hold of the class before storage and ultimate withdrawal.

Above: The Class 24 was divided into two subdivisions because of minor electrical differences, but this did not stop them from being regularly worked together in multiple. Class 24/1 No 24.081 stands on the west side of Crewe station with Class 24/0, No 24.035 on 4 March 1978. They are awaiting the all clear to run round the Chester line before coming back through the station on their way to work light to Stoke ready for Sunday ballast duties.

Left: Although now extinct as a class on the Scottish Region, the Highlands have gained years of faithful service from their Inverness based Class 24/1s. Here, one of the depots allocation, No 24.129, is seen preparing to depart from the Kyle of Lochalsh with the 11.08 service to Inverness. Since the disappearance of the class these duties, together with those to Wick and Thurso, have been taken over by Class 26s, many of which have been especially transferred from Haymarket for the job.

Right: Originally allocated to Gateshead depot in Newcastle, 10 Class 24/1s Nos 24.102-111 (formerly Nos 5102-11) were fitted with air pipe equipment and employed in pairs on the Tyne Dock to Consett block iron ore trains. Later, whilst allocated to Haymarket and with the air pipe equipment clearly visible above the buffer beam, No 24.110 leaves Millerhill yard on 20 April 1976 with the Leith South portion of the 6S41 09.05 Haverton Hill to Grangemouth.

Below: No doubt feeling very much at home with the semaphore signalling, Nos 24.079 and 24.087, both boiler fitted, are seen taking a breather at Shrewsbury on the outward journey of the Wirral Railway Circle's 'Cambrian Coast Express' on 20 March 1976. The train, the 09.12 Crewe to Pwllheli, enabled the participants to view the breath taking Cambrian Coast in loco hauled comfort. / *G. R. Hounsell*

Far right: Still carrying their original numbers, Class 24/1 Nos 5124 and 5129, (eventually to be renumbered 24.124 and 24.129), make a photographic stop at Dunrobin whilst en route from Inverness to Thurso and Wick with the Wirral Railway Circle's 'Great Briton Ltd' charter rail tour on Saturday 25 May 1974. / *G. R. Hounsell*

Bottom right: Later the same day Nos 5124 and 5129 are seen once more, this time awaiting departure from Georgemas Junction at 16.50 with the return charter to Inverness. / *G. R. Hounsell*

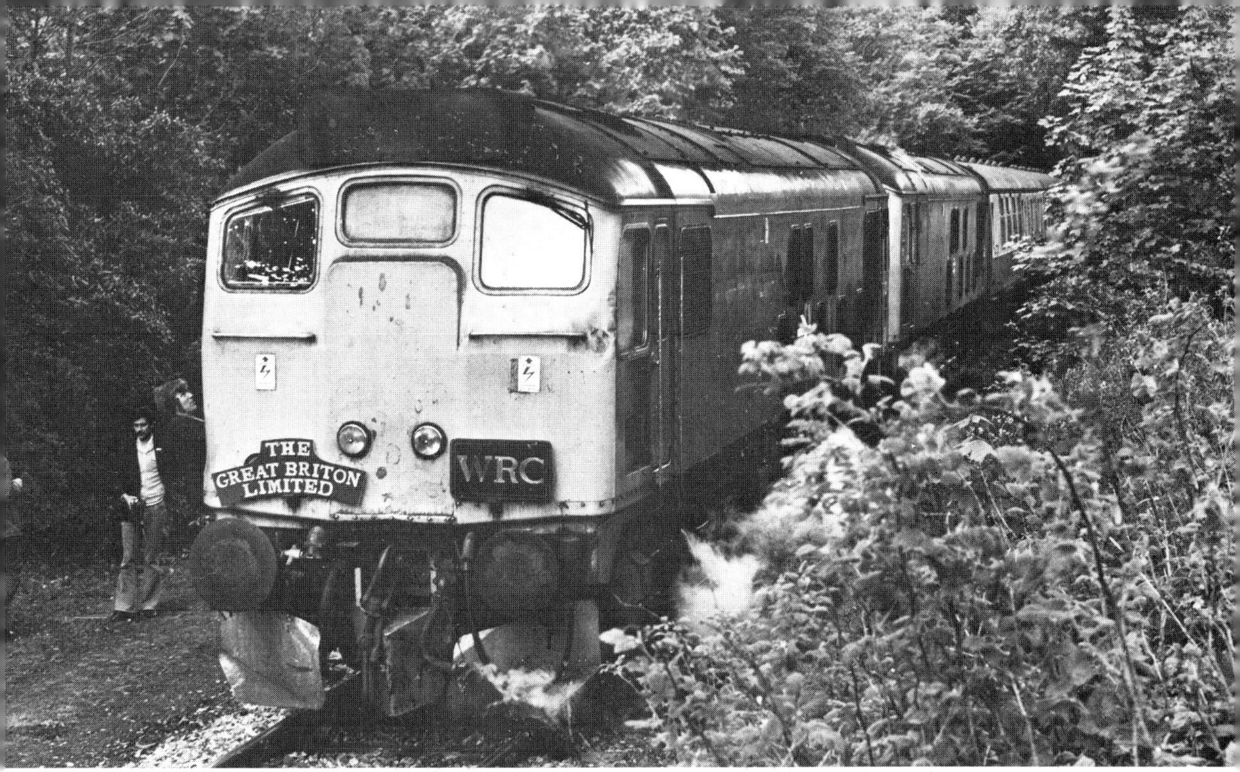
THE
GREAT BRITON
LIMITED
WRC

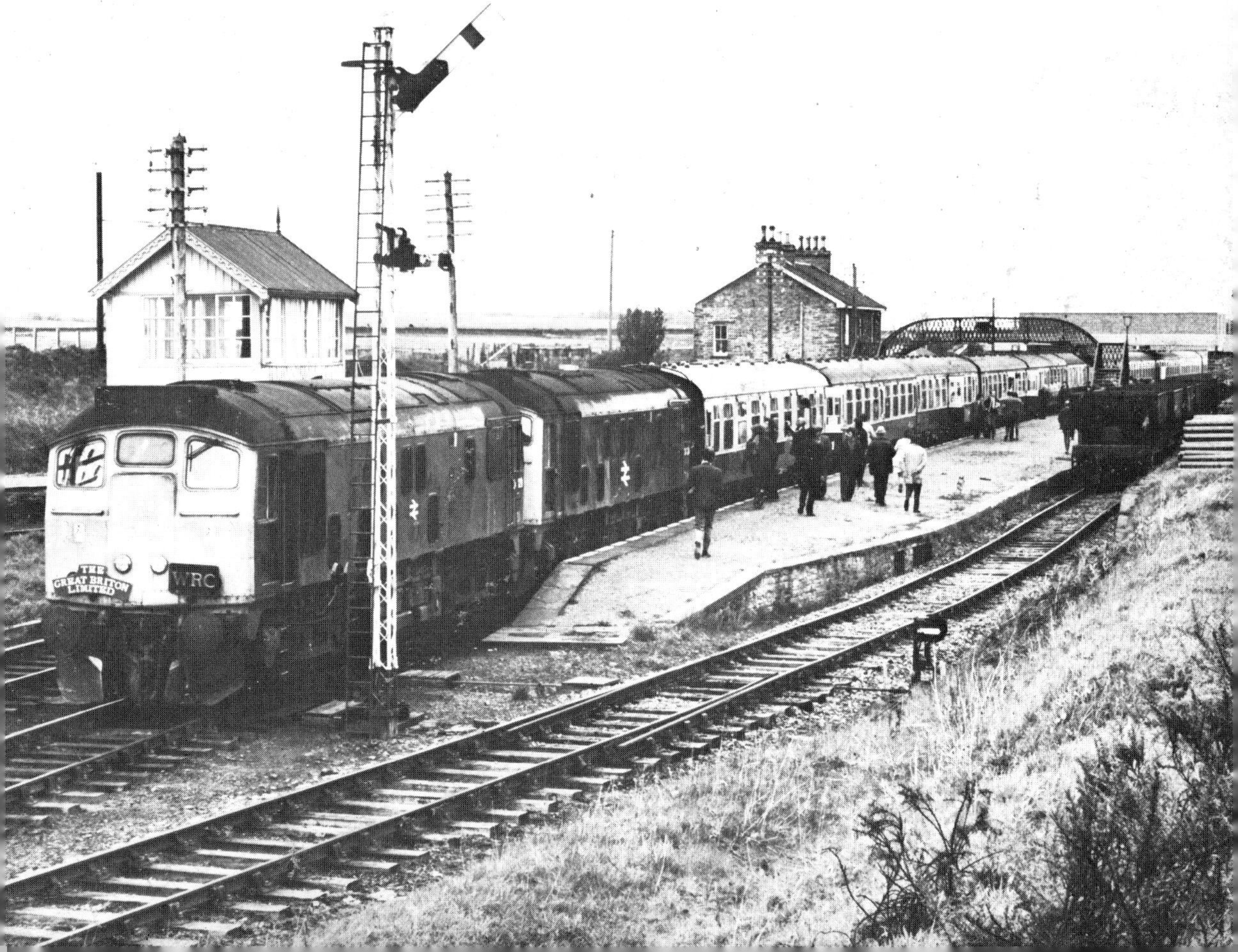
THE
GREAT BRITON
LIMITED
WRC

Below: On another Wirral Railway Circle special two of the last Crewe based boiler fitted Class 24s Nos 24.082 and 24.087 rattle through the site of the former Sheffield Victoria station with the Great Central excursion from Crewe to Loughborough on 4 December 1976. / *L. A. Nixon*

Bottom: Once they were condemned the London Midland Class 24/0s and 24/1s, all based at Crewe and Longsight in Manchester, were mostly stored at Basford Hall or Reddish pending disposal. They were then gradually moved, usually in batches of four as exceptional loads, to Swindon and later on to Doncaster Works to be cut up. No 24.058 was one of the first dozen locomotives to make its way to Swindon, and is seen in the main erecting shop having the combustible parts removed before being transferred to the dump. Any reusable parts were sent as a rule to Derby Works in En-parts vehicles for use on the Class 25s.

Class 25

Right: One of only 13 Class 25/0s left in service, No 25.008 pauses at Kirkaldy in Fife with 1G45 11.03 Perth to Edinburgh Waverley on Saturday 29 July 1978. Most of the remaining members of the class have recently undergone intermediate overhauls, although this particular specimen has still to go through the works.

Below: Prior to their transfer from Tinsley on the Eastern Region to the Scottish Region, Nos 25.033 and 25.023 are seen working in multiple on 11 June 1974. They are powering the 7V61 Bescot to Severn Tunnel Junction freight southwards through Cheltenham as they pass a 'Peak' class on a Manchester train.

VB(EQ)	Class	25-2
Weight tons		74
Brake force tons		38
RA		5
Max speed mph		90

Tinsley **TI**

**BRITISH RAILWAYS
DERBY BUILT**
1963
POWER EQUIPMENT BY
ASSOCIATED ELECTRICAL INDUSTRIES LTD
AND SULZER

Right: Close-up of cab-side details on No 25.092 whilst the locomotive was allocated to Plymouth Laira, although at the time still sporting a Tinsley depot allocation sticker.

Below: Nos 25.107 and 25.123 prepare to leave Norwich depot on Saturday 21 August 1976 to work light to Yarmouth after being fuelled and examined. Class 25s, although not common in East Anglia, are quite often seen at Whitemoor. This pair is programmed to arrive at Yarmouth with a train from Derby and leave with another for Walsall near Birmingham.

Above: Shortly after returning from Royal Train duties, Nos 25.057 and 25.218 await fuelling on Crewe holding sidings on 27 April 1977. Since May 1978 No 25.057 has been transferred to Plymouth Laira and works out of St Blazey or Exeter, mainly on china clay work.

Left: Eastfield based Class 25/2 No 25.108 prepares to depart from Rannoch station on the West Highland line with the 1T45 12.50 Mallaig to Glasgow Queen Street via Fort William. Although the train is obviously ready to depart the signal had not been cleared because the 8B13 12.58 Cadder yard to Corpach pulp mill freight, running approximately an hour early, was due to cross it at this point.

Top left: During its allocation to Bristol Bath Road MPD on the Western Region, No 25.156 passes under East Gantry with the 2B32 12.45 Cardiff Central to Taunton on 3 July 1975. Although the service was normally booked for, and worked by, a dmu it was poor availability that allowed a locomotive and coaches to be run in lieu on this occasion.

Left: Nos 25.088 and 25.314, both fitted with snowplough brackets to which miniature snowploughs may be attached during the winter months, make their way towards Salop Goods Junction before descending the Manchester independent line at Crewe with 4F53 14.30 Forders sidings to Garston, Fletliner Brick train on 25 May 1977. This service is one of only a few that travel long distances under the wires, but are diesel hauled throughout. The train stops at Basford Hall for train crew purposes, and on the left the relieved driver can be seen next to the diesel depot, on his way to book off.

Top: The 8L15 12.55 Oakamoor to Ravenhead St Helens sandhopper freight winds its way through Crewe after leaving the Stoke line with Nos 25.295 and 25.184 in charge. Subsequent to the photograph being taken, the leading locomotive, No 25.295, was involved in a collision in the London area, causing enough accident damage for it to be written off and scrapped on 10 June 1978.

Above: No 25.224 hurries through the Cheshire country side with the mid-afternoon Crewe to Cardiff locomotive hauled service on 17 June 1978. The photograph, taken near Nantwich, shows a somewhat larger than usual formation with no less than eight vehicles instead of the usual six. No 25.224 was one of the three Class 25s transferred from the Western Region to Crewe to replace three dual-braked specimens sent to Plymouth Laira in May 1978.

Above: No 25.108 makes its way slowly south from Corrour towards Rannoch with the mid-afternoon service from Mallaig to Glasgow Queen Street. It is one of only three non-boilered Class 25/2s allocated to the Scottish Region, and normally only seen on passenger turns during the summer months. Seven of these locomotives are allocated to Eastfield whilst the balance belong to Haymarket.

Top right: The 4K53 17.55 parcels from Bangor stands in Crewe station shortly after arrival behind No 25.056 on 21 February 1977. Once the vans have been emptied by station and post office staff they are propelled into Up Hill sidings where a Class 08 remarshals them into a Euston bound train.

Right: Although Plymouth Laira is the only Western Region depot still retaining a somewhat depleted allocation of Class 25s, they are by no means rare elsewhere on the region. Here Nos 25.270 and 25.107, both allocated to Toton, stand in Alstone sidings with the stock from the 1Z49 06.18 excursion from Nelson in Lancashire to Cheltenham on 20 May 1978.

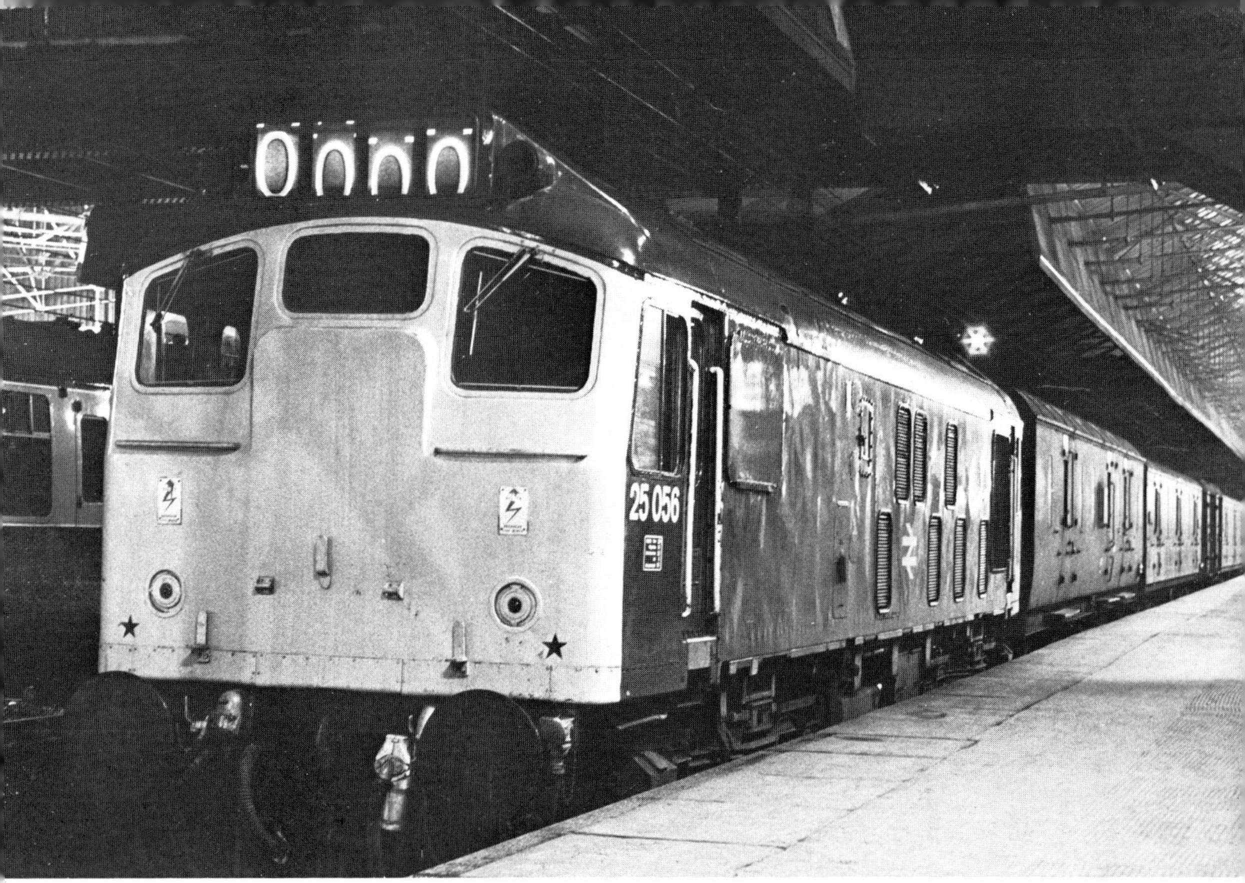
0000
25 056

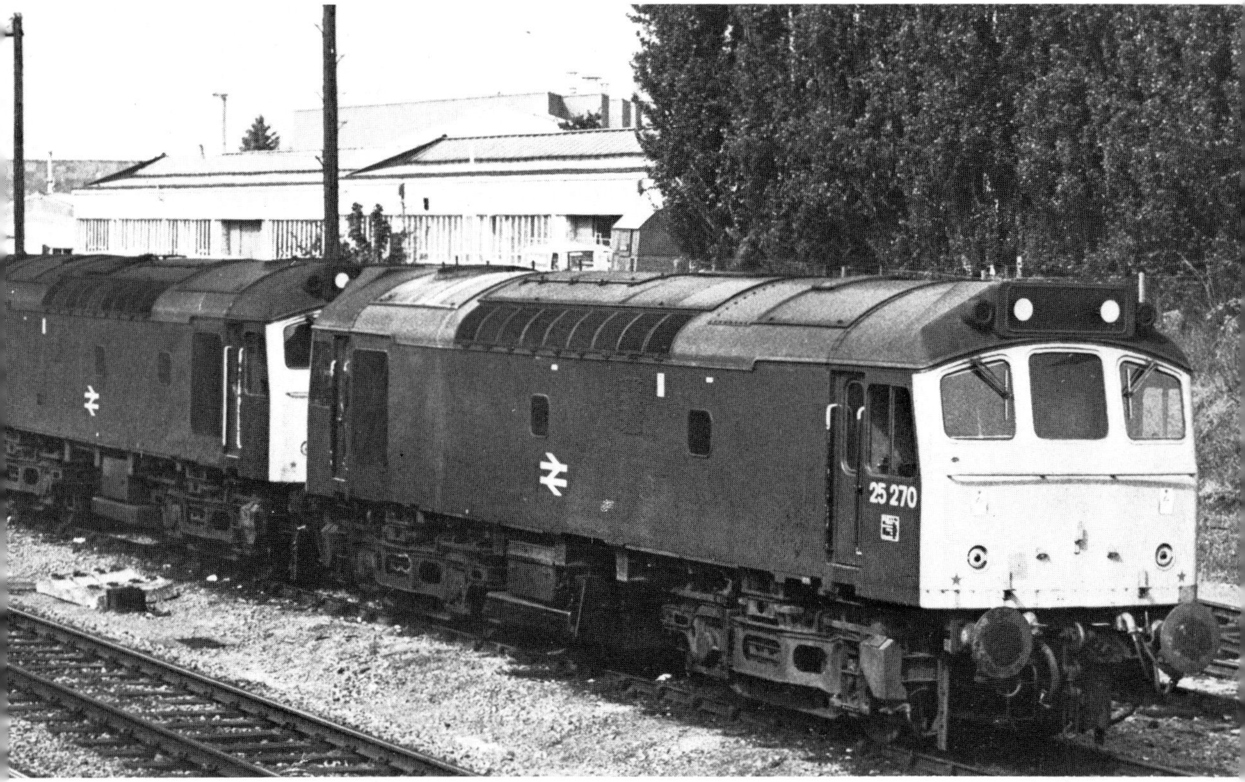
25 270

Below: Two Class 25/3s stand buffer to buffer on Crewe holding siding on 9 August 1978. No 25.270 is one of the class to be renumbered incorrectly because the left hand cab side which should carrry the number bears the cab indentation which once housed the token pick-up equipment.

Class 26

Top: A study of No 26.006 standing in Haymarket station on 30 March 1975. This particular locomotive is one of only seven Class 26/0 locomotives fitted with dual brakes and slow speed running control to enable them to unload MGR coal freights, usually in Fife power stations. Although the remainder of the class are all allocated to Inverness these seven specimens have been retained at Haymarket because of their modifications.

Above: A Class 26/0 and 26/1 pose side by side on Perth stabling point. The two subdivisions have only minor external differences which include buffers, cab windows and the position of multiple working jumper cables. Only the Class 26/1s have brackets to enable miniature snowploughs to be attached.

Left: Nos 26.028 and 26.024 run into Pitlochry station past the head porter on the evening of 28 July 1978 with an Inverness bound passenger train. When the class were renumbered most locomotives traded the 53 part of their number for 260, but in the case of the leading locomotive, originally No 5320, this was not the case because in order to keep the subdivisions apart it moved to the slot 5328 would have taken had it not been withdrawn several years earlier because of severe collision damage.

Below: Blair Atholl, at the most southerly end of the recently reinstated double line section from Dalwhinnie, prepares for the arrival of Nos 26.023 and 26.033 with the 1N32 13.10 Glasgow Queen Street to Inverness service on 26 July 1978.

Right: Sporting newly painted miniature snowploughs, No 26.025 recently out-shopped from Glasgow Works accelerates its way north out of Pitlochry station with No 26.045 on the 1N36 17.35 Edinburgh Waverley to Inverness service. To the right, just in front of the signalbox, holiday makers await the passage of the train before crossing the track from the Salmon Ladder to the town centre.

Below right: Nos 26.026 and 26.035 make a quick, if not particularly clean get away from Perth with the 1T20 08.15 Inverness to Glasgow Queen Street service on Saturday 29 July 1978. In the background passengers are seen boarding the 11.03 departure which forms a connection to Edinburgh.

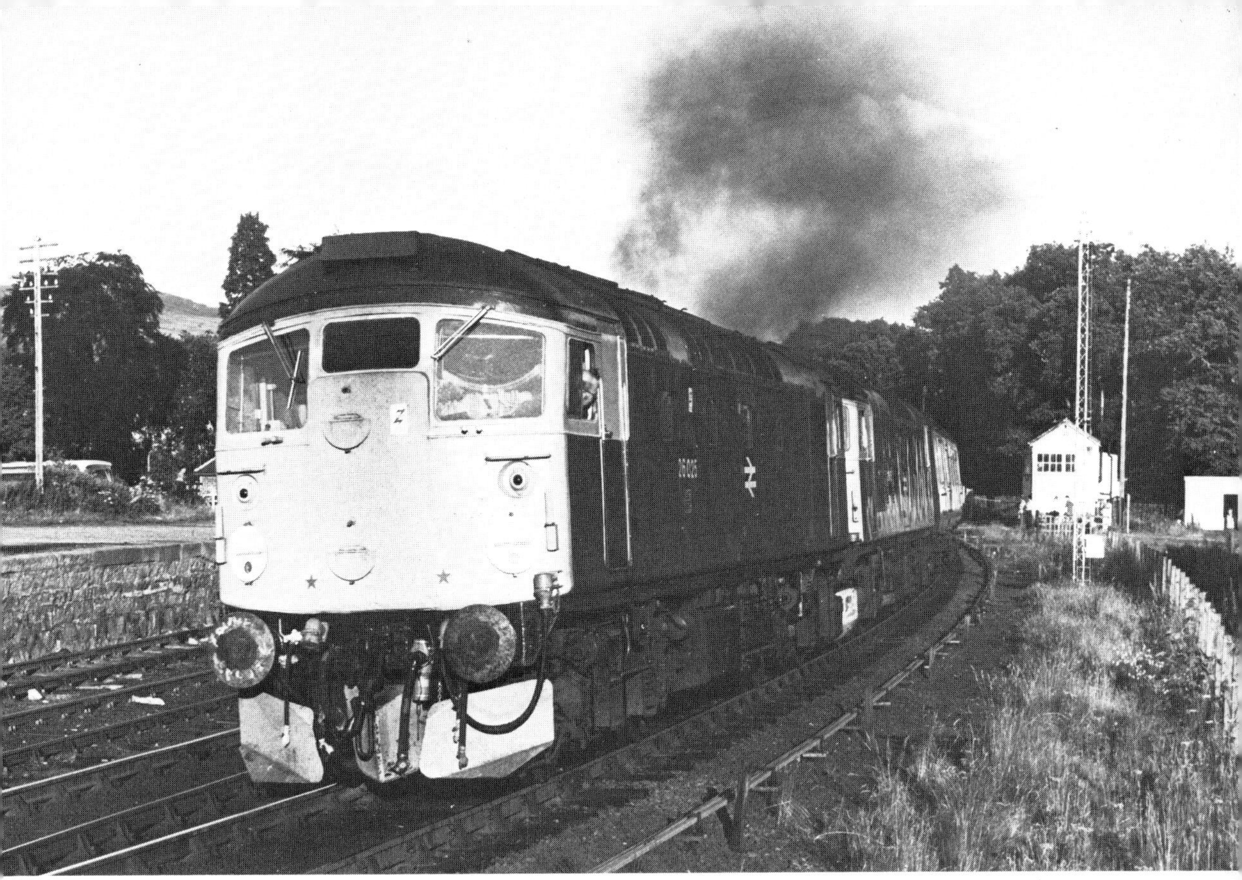

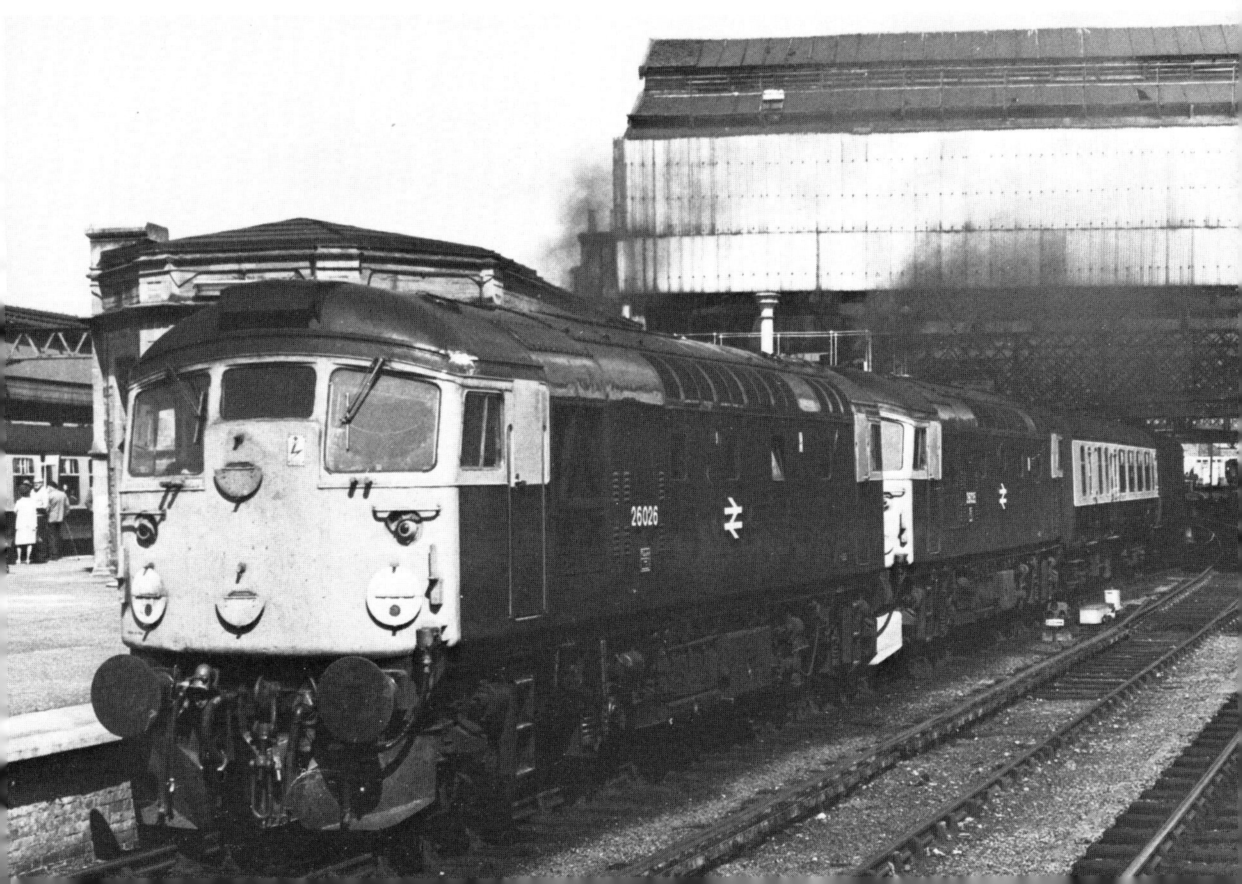
26026

Above: An evening Edinburgh Waverley to Inverness train runs into Perth behind Nos 26.025 and 26.045. The train, although booked for this type of traction, is quite often powered by larger locomotives such as Classes 40 and 47.

Right: On 1 August 1978 Nos 26.031 and 26.032 appeared to be making light work of the 1T20 08.15 Inverness to Glasgow Queen Street as they sped towards Ballinluig. Unfortunately, the lack of noise obviously heralded a problem. Instead of returning later in the day they had to go on to Eastfield MPD for attention, and were substituted by a Class 47.

Top right: A trio of Class 26s stand on Perth stabling point on Saturday, 29 July 1978. On the left, Class 26/0 No 26.010, sporting oval buffers, stands next to No 26.026, whilst on the right, No 26.035 is fitted with snowploughs and sealed beam headlights. The lattter are for use at night, usually north of Inverness, as a warning in particular to sheep.

Far right: Preparing to make the initial journey back to its home maintenance depot at Inverness, No 26.027 is seen standing in Glasgow Queen Street station on 28 March 1975, after undergoing a general overhaul in the nearby Glasgow St Rollox Works. At one time the entire class were fitted with token pick-up equipment, but in recent years this has become obsolete and has been removed to enable the indentation to be covered over thereby giving a better profile.

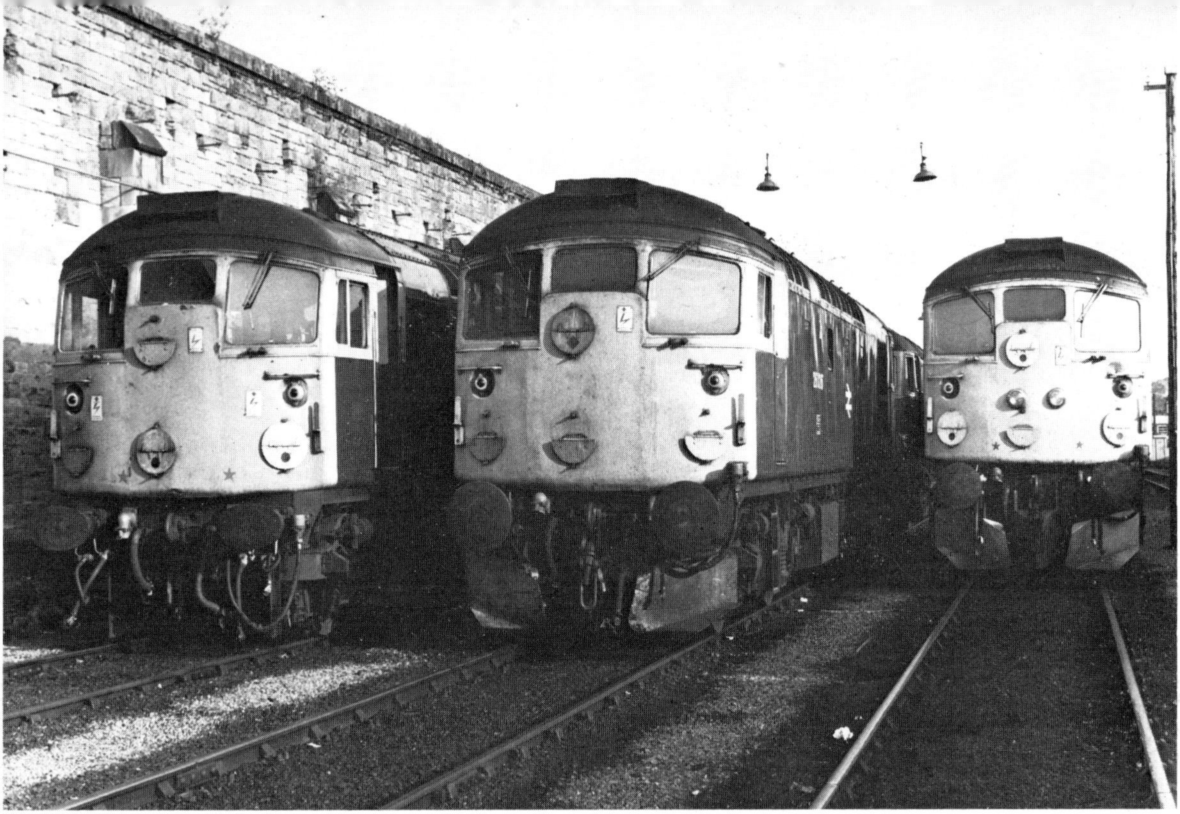

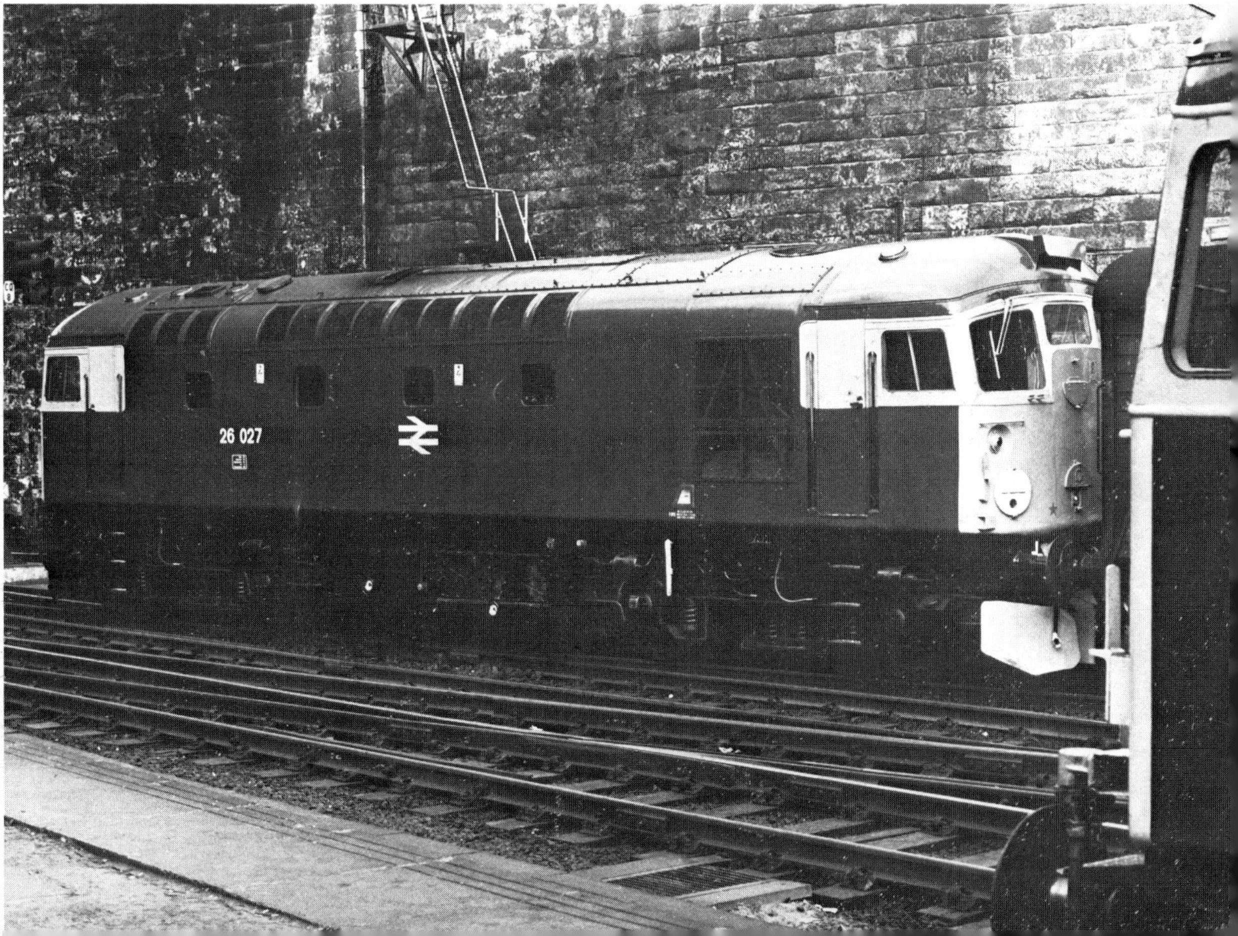
26 027

Above: Eastfield depot in Scotland has an allocation of both classes 25 and 27 Type 2 locomotives, although on 24 May 1975 an Inverness Class 26 was also present. From right to left the traction 'on shed' were: Nos 26.030, 27.106, 27.035 and 25.226, whilst No 27.104 sped past at the rear of an Edinburgh to Glasgow high speed service.

Right: No 26.027 runs into Helmsdale station, south of Georgemas Junction, on 30 May 1977 with the 2K09 11.10 Inverness to Wick and Thurso. As it does so the driver hangs out of the locomotive's cab window with his token in readiness to swap it with the stationmaster, for that of the next section. / *B. Morrison*

Class 27

Above: Whilst soaking up the summer sunshine on 28 May 1977, No 27.007 is seen working the 2T46 17.38 Dundee to Glasgow Queen Street service through Forteviot, just south of Perth. / *B. Morrison*

Below: Class 27/0 No 27.015 approaches Stirling on 23 May 1976 with the 17.35 Glasgow Queen Street to Dundee service. Unfortunately owing to extensive fire damage this particular locomotive was put into store on 17 January 1977 and finally withdrawn from service 10 days later on 27 January. / *B. Morrison*

Below: 27.038, again fitted with dual brakes, makes its way towards Rannoch station from the south with the 8B13 12.58 SX Cadder to Corpach pulp mill freight, running over an hour early. Consequently it was able to cross the up Mallaig to Glasgow passenger train at Rannoch and then proceed unhindered to its destination.

Bottom: One of only four Class 27/0s to be fitted with dual brakes during their last main works general overhauls, No 27.034 makes its way tentatively south along the single track from Currour towards Rannoch. It is seen in the beautiful West Highland countryside on 31 July 1978, hauling 6D12 13.14 SX air-braked service from Mallaig Junction yard near Fort William to Mossend.

Below: A study of Class 27/0 No 27.042 outside its home maintenance depot, Eastfield. Several members of the class have been withdrawn from service but only when accident or fire damage has proved too costly to effect repairs.

Bottom: Although all Class 27 locomotives are capable of being fitted with miniature snowploughs, obviously only a certain number carry them at any one time, particularly during the summer months. On this occasion the driver of No 27.041 has his token ready to hand in at Rannoch as he runs into the station with 6D13 15.52 Mallaig Junction Yard to Mossend air-braked service. On occasions this train conveys mails from Fort William to Crianlarich but on this occasion did not appear to be doing so.

Left: The 1035 14.30 high speed service from Glasgow Queen Street runs into Edinburgh Waverley station in the hands of two boiler fitted Class 27/1s. At the front and furthest away from the camera is No 27.102, whilst at the rear 27.101 holds the fort.

Right: No 27.201 stands in Glasgow Queen Street station on 30 March 1975 with the 14.00 departure for Edinburgh. Originally renumbered No 27.119, it was the first Class 27 to have its boiler removed and be fitted with electric train heating (ETH), to enable the introduction of the high speed service between Scotland's two main cities Glasgow and Edinburgh.

Below: The Edinburgh and Glasgow high speed services are programmed to be worked by two Class 27/2 locomotives, but inevitably Class 27/1s have to be substituted for failures when poor availability dictates. Here No 27.111 fitted with dual brakes and a train heating boiler, prepares to assist from the rear of the 1031 13.30 high speed service from Glasgow Queen Street to Edinburgh out of Haymarket station, on the final leg of its $47\frac{1}{4}$-mile journey.

Above: Shortly after leaving Haymarket station, Nos 27.201 and 27.210, the latter assisting at the rear, cross Haymarket East Junction with the 1036 14.00 Edinburgh Waverley to Glasgow Queen Street service. The class 27/2s are the only Type 2 locomotives, apart from Western and Eastern Region Class 31/4s, to be modified and fitted with electric train heating equipment.

Left: No 27.103 makes rather dirty work of leading the 1042 15.00 Edinburgh to Glasgow service out of Waverley station on 29 July 1978, whilst No 27.209 assists at the rear. Originally numbered 5413 and renumbered 27.118, the leading locomotive was due to undergo an electric train heat modification and become 27.212. However, eventually No 5386 (formerly renumbered 27.103) was modified, and so two locomotives have carried the number 27.103, but never at the same time.

Class 31

Right: Immaculately turned out by Stratford depot staff Nos 31.005 and 31.019, still fitted with operative boilers, cross Cheltenham Road viaduct near Montpellier, Bristol with the 08.03 'Toffee Apple' special railtour from Paddington to Portishead and Tytherington via Avonmouth on 22 October 1977. / *G. R. Hounsell*

Below: Study of a Class 31/0, No 31.009, fitted with red circle electro-magnetic multiple working controls, on Stratford diesel depot. This class subdivision, once totalling 19 but now reduced to nine has, (with the exception of No 31.004), so far spent its entire renumbered life at Stratford, East London. During its absence No 31.004 was allocated to March for a number of months in 1975.

Top left: Immingham based Class 31/1 No 31.324, crosses Manningtree south viaduct on 21 May 1976 with the 16.52 service from Peterborough to Parkeston Quay. The train will shortly be leaving the Great Eastern main line and will take the Harwich branch. / G. R. Mortimer

Centre left: One of Gateshead's dozen or so Class 31/1s is seen south of the depot on 6 April 1977, working a local trip to Tyne Yard. It is conveying sand in unfitted mineral wagons and this particular locomotive is fitted with vacuum brakes only and has had its steam generator removed.

Bottom left: Class 31/0 No 31.008 hauls a ballast dropping train over a stretch of newly laid track to the north of Manningtree on Sunday 3 August 1975. The driver's assistant leans out of the locomotive's window to keep an eye on proceedings and give the 'all clear' once all the ballast has been dropped. / G. R. Mortimer

Above: No 31.166 with a modified headcode panel, rumbles over Shireoaks East Junction on 30 May 1978. The locomotive is hauling the 8T61 trip from Rotherwood to Worksop which on this occasion was running as a fully fitted Class 6 freight.

Right: The driver of Finsbury Park's No 31.220 reads his newspaper while awaiting departure from Kings Cross for Holloway carriage sidings with the ECS off the down 'Aberdonian'. Above the locomotive the relatively new and most distinctive station canopy is clearly visible.

41

Above: Until the Great Northern electrification almost all services to and from Cambridge to Kings Cross were worked by Class 31/1s, normally allocated to either Finsbury Park, March or, on rarer occasions, Stratford. The mid-afternoon service on Saturday 17 August 1974 was in the hands of No 31.188 as it rolled into Kings Cross five minutes early.

Right: A close up of an early member of the Class 31/1 subdivision showing all the details inherent from the prototype locomotives. This particular locmotive, No 31.121, is fitted with dual brakes and an operative steam generator. It has also retained the connecting doors on the front, but will no doubt have them welded up when it next goes through works for a general overhaul.

Above: Class 31 locomotives are regularly used to work parcel trains on the Eastern and Western Regions. No 31.241 had just arrived in Bristol Temple Meads with the 4B05 05.05 express parcels from Paddington when it was captured on film on 21 May 1976.

Left: After its number four traction motor had ceased whilst working between Bristol and Keynsham on 26 July 1976, No 31.315 (allocated to March) was hauled into Bristol Bath Road motive power depot. Here, on 28 July under the supervision of the depot engineer, the locomotive was lifted with the aid of the diesel crane and hydraulic jacks, to enable the defective traction motor to be removed and replaced by a brand new one.

Above: No 31.416 stands inside Old Oak Common fuel point on 3 November 1973 shortly after being renumbered. This particular locomotive is fitted with both a steam generator and electric train heating equipment.

Right: Finsbury Park allocated Class 31/4 No 31.403 leaves Kings Cross on the summer morning of 12 June 1975 with the empty carriage stock off an overnight train from the Scottish Region. At the time the shot was taken, work was still in progress on the station canopy and in consequence the scaffolding was still in situ. / *B. Morrison*

Class 33

Right: Eastleigh based Class 33 No 33.006 makes its way slowly under Star Bridge near Hooley, with the 14.55 trip freight from Norwood Yard to Merstham Yard on 20 April 1976. / *J. Scrace*

Below: The driver of No 33.024 prepares to board his locomotive on 9 April 1974 in readiness to work the 07.00 Newcastle to Poole service forward from Reading. The train arrived behind an LMR ETH-fitted Class 47. In recent years the Class 33s have become progressively more rare on this final leg of the journey.

Above The 11.00 Waterloo to Exeter service runs out of Vauxhall station shortly after leaving the capital on 18 September 1978 in the very capable hands of No 33.026. / *J. Scrace*

Left: No 33.031 approaches Dundonald road crossing Wimbledon with a 13.05 special conveying empty coal hoppers to Betteshanger Colliery on 11 June 1974. The train originated from the local coal concentration depot. / *J. Scrace*

Top right: No 33.051, allocated to Hither Green diesel depot, stands at North Kent West Junction on 6 August 1974 with the 12.13 freight from Norwood Yard to Hoo Junction. To the left of the train is one of the Class 73 electro-diesels, the only such class now left on the Southern Region. / *J. Scrace*

Right: Class 31/1 No 33.107 basks in the summer sun whilst waiting at Weymouth Quay with the 15.50 Boat Train service to Waterloo on 1 July 1974. / *B. Morrison*

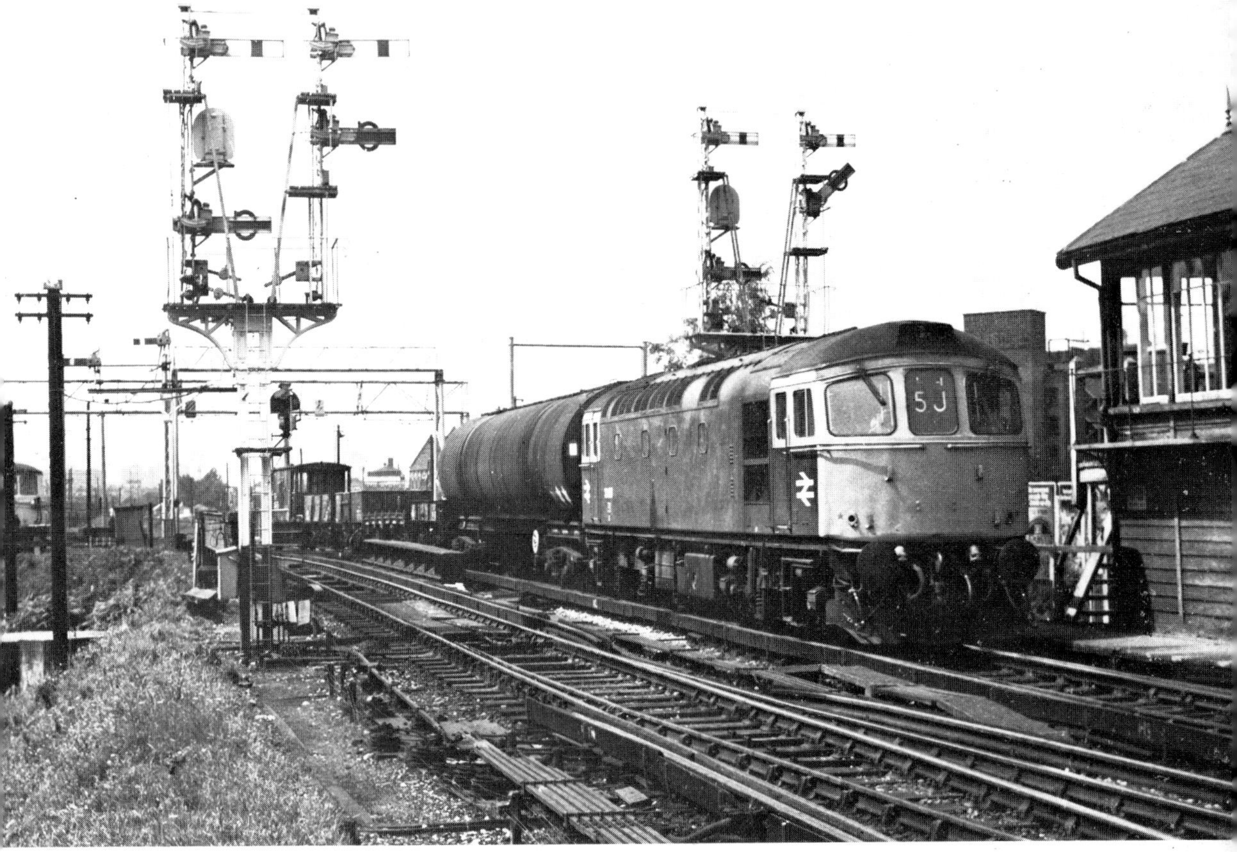
5J

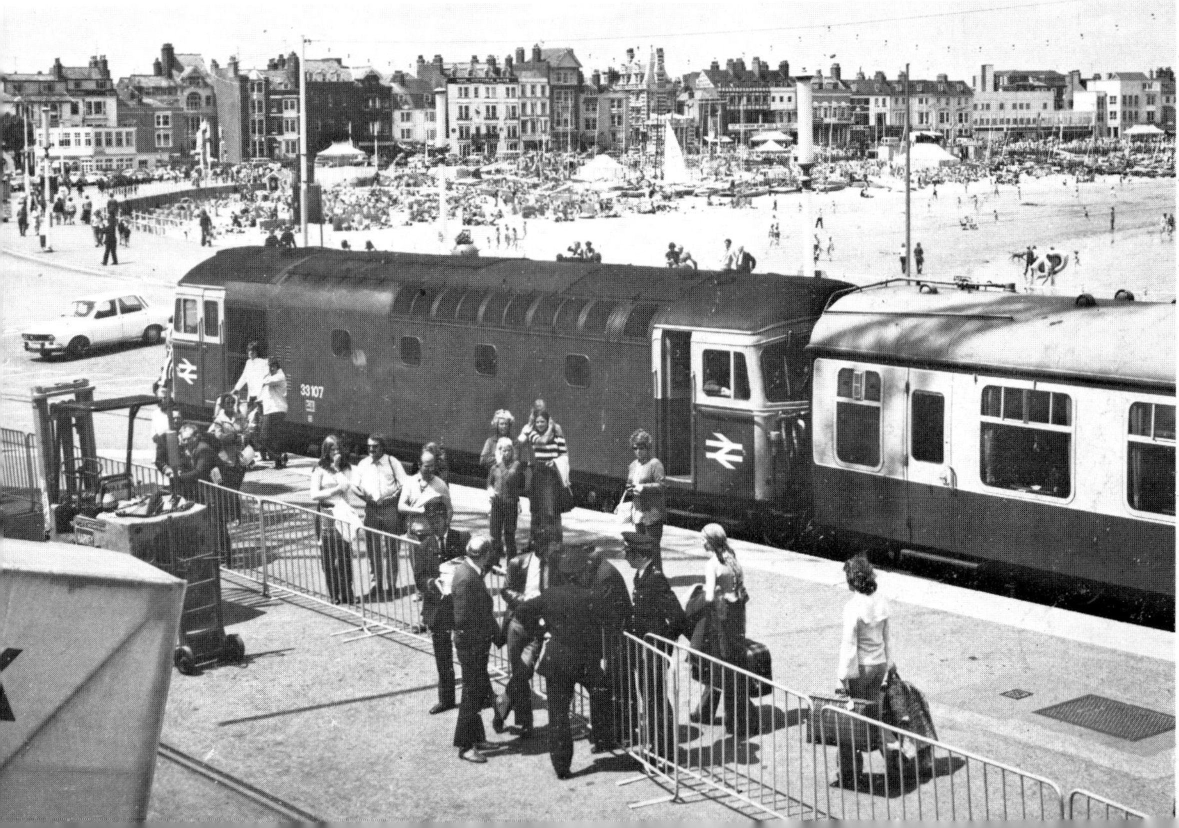
33107

Above: A number of years ago 19 of the Eastleigh based Class 33s were fitted with emu push/pull working. They were converted for use between Bournemouth and Weymouth, and this meant that when coupled to a 4TC unit, they could be driven from either end of the train. The equipment is clearly visible on this close up of No 33.101 standing in Reading station in April 1974.

Centre left: Although fitted with push/pull equipment, Class 33/1s can turn their arm to any kind of duty. Here, No 33.107 crosses North Somerset Junction on 20 May 1975 with the 7C46 13.05 SX Westbury to Margam coal empties.

Bottom left: No 6588, (since renumbered 33.203), makes its way from the Southern to the London Midland Region via the cross London lines on 15 June 1973. The locomotive, one of 12 fitted with slow speed running control and built with slab sides to conform with the Hastings line loading gauge, heads the 13.32 Hoo Junction to Thame conditional block oil freight through West Brompton. / *J. Scrace*

Top right: On 2 April 1974 No 33.114 was in charge of the 07.00 service from Newcastle to Poole as it departed from Southampton. In the background the outer extremities of the once thriving dock complex can be seen, where the Eastleigh based Class 07 Ruston and Hornsby shunt engines were used until the end of 1977. / *J. Scrace*

Right: No 33.008 moves slowly out of Exeter St Davids station with the 15.55 afternoon service to Waterloo on 21 July 1977. The locomotive is fitted with miniature snowploughs and is one of 33 Class 33/0s allocated to Eastleigh near Southampton on the Southern Region. / *B. Morrison*

Right: No 33.205 is one of only 12 Class 33/2s all allocated to Hither Green MPD and is seen approaching Stone crossing with a Mountfield to Northfleet gypsum freight on 29 March 1978. / *B. Morrison*

Below: Class 33/2 No 33.202, once again built to the Hastings line loading gauge, crosses Chelsea Bridge with a train of Conoco tanks from the Western Region to Strood sidings via Kensington and Sidcup on 25 May 1977. / *B. Morrison*

Class 37

Above: Class 37 No 37.041, allocated to March TMD, is seen about to cross the River Ouse near Ely with the 17.24 Kings Lynn to Cambridge and London Liverpool Street on Saturday 3 April 1976. / *G. R. Hounsell*

Below: No 37.055, with its destination blinds replaced by dots and looking somewhat cross-eyed, is seen shortly after emerging from under Redheugh road bridge with a cement Presflo train bound for Ferryhill.

Left: Any form of Class 37 is a rare sight at Crewe, but the appearance of an Eastern Region outside headcode specimen on a passenger train on 15 April 1978 was even more so. No 37.026 awaits departure from platform 4B with the 2V67 10.00 Crewe to Cardiff service, before the trains were up graded to Class 1 timings at the start of the 1978/1979 timetable.

Above: Thornaby based Class 37 No 37.119, formerly 6700, rumbles through the Cotswold countryside on Tuesday 10 February 1976 with the 6Z62 19.40 (of Monday) Tyne to Severn Beach anhydrous ammonia control special comprising four barrier wagons (two at each end) 23 vacuum braked tanks and a dual-piped brake van.

Right: No 37.083 approaches Cloddy Moor footbridge on 3 June 1974 with the 8V77 11.35 SX conditional freight from Toton to Severn Tunnel Junction. This locomotive is one of 119 such locomotives to be built with outside headcodes, although three have now had the boxes modified following accident damage. These are: Nos 37.073, 37.074 and 37.091 which all underwent the alteration whilst undergoing repair.

Above: One of March depots cleaner Class 37s No 37.051 passes slowly through Sproughton, to the north of Ipswich, with a train of 45-tonne tanks from North Walsham to Parkeston on 28 July 1978. The reason for the locomotive's cleanliness is due to the fact that it recently underwent an overhaul and dual brake conversion in Doncaster Works. / *G. R. Mortimer*

Left: A rather grimy Welsh based Class 37 No 37.175, fitted with a boiler and miniature snowploughs, makes light work of the six-coach 2V67 12.22 Crewe to Cardiff service as it moves swiftly towards Willaston on 17 February 1978.

Top right: Although for a short spell several years ago Western Region Class 37s were overhauled in Crewe Works, it has normally been Doncaster's prerogative to maintain the entire fleet. On 7 April 1974 No 37.187 fitted with a boiler and allocated to Landore, was photographed whilst undergoing a general overhaul in Doncaster Works.

Right: No 37.166, freshly out shopped from Doncaster Works, poses on Bristol Bath Road diesel depot, before entering the fuelling point for an examination on 9 June 1976.

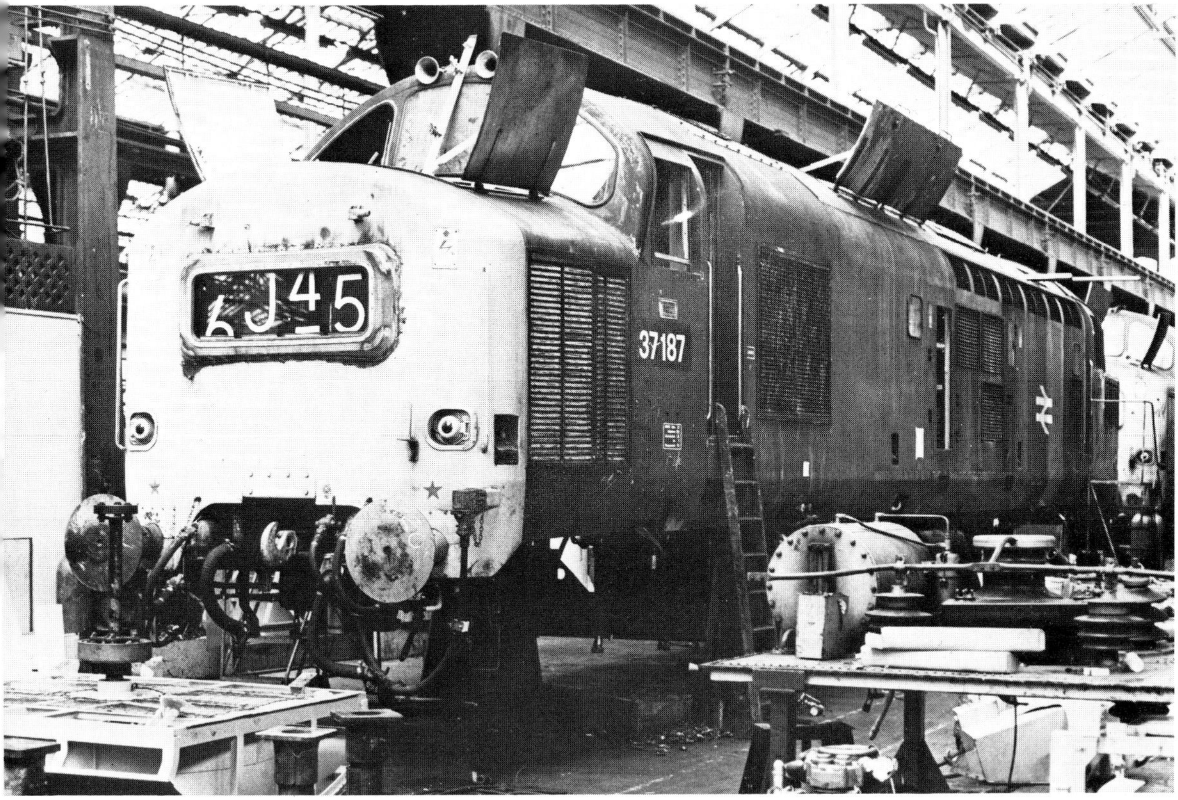
6J45
37187

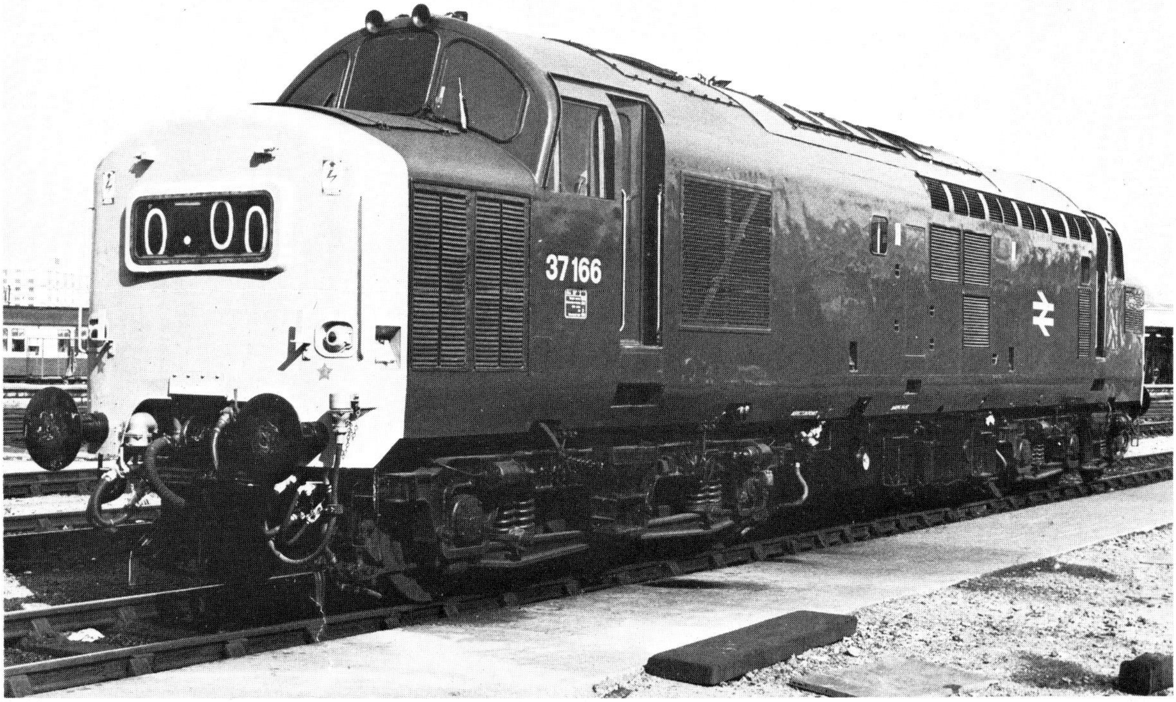
0.00
37166

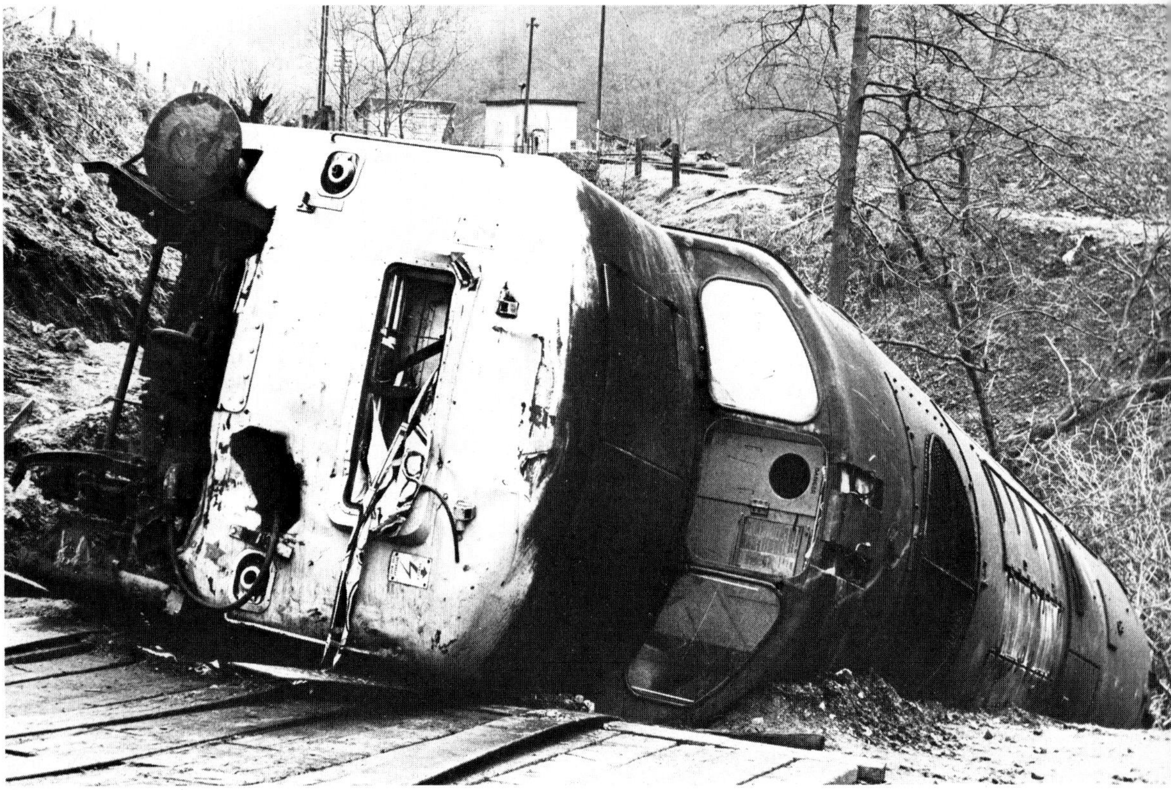

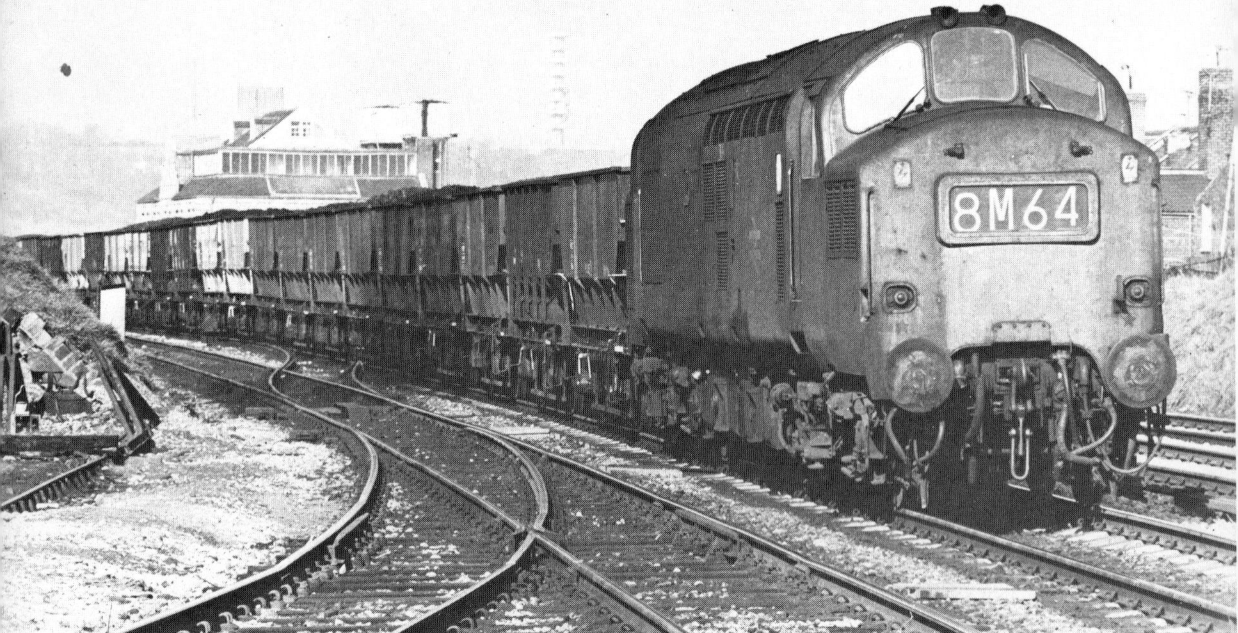
8M64

Left: Accidents will always happen however careful one is. Here No 37.143 is seen down an embankment at the most southerly end of Marine Colliery in South Wales after coming to grief at the head of an unfitted coal train in January 1975. This shot was, in fact, taken on 15 March, and the locomotive remained unmoved for a further few months before being returned to the British Rail network by the gentle persuasion of No 1200 *Falcon*, amongst other motive power.

Bottom left: A filthy engine, No 37.179, descends Filton Bank with a train of coal hoppers bound for Wapping Wharf coal concentration depot near Bristol. The British Railways insignia is vaguely discernible through the grime on the locomotive's side, and the once yellow nose now affords little warning to those working on the track.

Right: Stratford East London based No 37.261, one of the first 10 Class 37s to be fitted with dual brakes, speeds southwards through Tivetshall on the Great Eastern main line with the 10.50 summer Saturday only service from Yarmouth to London Liverpool Street, on 28 May 1977. / G. R. Mortimer

Below: Nos 37.209 and 37.128, both allocated to Tinsley depot in Sheffield, ease their way out of Worksop Yard with a train of empty merry-go-round hoppers bound for Manton Colliery several miles to the east on 30 May 1978.

Top: Substituting for the regular dmu service, No 37.253 heads the 13.15 2B32 Cardiff to Taunton five-coach train past Victoria Park on the south-west side of Bristol on 9 August 1976. As this particular locomotive is not fitted with a boiler, it was only used because being August the train did not require heating.

Above: No 37.288, allocated to Canton depot Cardiff, pauses in Radyr station for a crew change on Sunday 21 July 1974, before being accepted into the yard for traffic purposes. The freight originated from Britannia Colliery and collected the oil tank on the journey south.

Class 40

Top: London Midland based Class 40s Nos 40.003 and 40.076 stand on Garston Dock stabling point on the afternoon the 26 April 1974 only several months before it was officially closed. Although both locomotives appear to be dual braked only the right hand one has under gone the works modification and one can only assume that No 40.003, now allocated to the Eastern Region, had had a depot bogie change and the air brake pipes had not been removed.

Above: No 40.006 recently transferred back to Healey Mills depot, speeds along the coast north of Carnoustie at East Haven on 28 July 1978 with the 1T27 11.17 Aberdeen to Glasgow Queen Street. Although none of the class is programmed to passenger work on the Scottish Region, it is not uncommon to see them substituting for Class 47s, particularly in the summer months.

ft: No 40.015, once named *Aquitania*, runs into ...hester on Saturday 3 June 1978 with 1K28 ...15 SO summer-dated Holyhead to Crewe ...rvice. Several weeks after this photograph was ...ken the engine entered Crewe Works for a ...neral overhaul and repaint.

elow left: Until fairly recently named *Empress ...' England*, No 40.033 makes its way towards ...resty No 1 signalbox, after a crew change, ...th the 6J41 12.04 TThO Moston Sidings to ...ayston Hill CCE depot empty ballast hopper ...eight. The driver and guard, who brought the ...ain from the Manchester Division on 5 May ...978, are seen making their way to the train ...ew hut for a physical needs break before ...turning home later in the afternoon.

ight: No 40.122, originally numbered D200, ...ttles through Willaston south of Crewe on ... May 1978 with a train of empty ballast ...oppers destined for the London Midland ...egion Quarry at Bayston Hill.

elow: The afternoon air brake network service ...om Whitemoor Yard to Parkeston Quay ...akes its way slowly along the Harwich branch ...n 15 Septmeber 1977 with Longsights ...o 40.119 in charge. It is seen at Warbness ...everal miles from its ultimate destination.
G. R. Mortimer

Top left: Study of vacuum braked Class 40 No 40.190, on its home maintenance depot, Wigan Spring Branch on 23 March 1975. Unfortunately, the locomotive, which had had its boiler isolated, was withdrawn from service on 31 January 1976 after spending several months in store pending a works estimate for extensive accident damage, sustained in a collision near Wigan.

Left: Vacuum braked Class 40 No 40.046 trundles southwards through Doncaster station with a train of unfitted 16-ton mineral wagons and 21-ton hoppers on 7 May 1974. No 40.046 is fitted with modified sanding gear to try to eliminate wheel slip and has, therefore spent its most recent years allocated to Healey Mills depot near Wakefield so that its specialised equipment can be monitored.

Above: One of 20 Class 40s fitted with outside headcode boxes and connecting doors in their noses, No 40.131 makes its way from Basford Hall towards Salop Goods signalbox and the ascent up the independent lines to Chester. The locomotive is working the 4D58 15.30 SX Lawley Street, in Birmingham, to Mold Junction Freightliner which on 18 May 1977 was extended through to Holyhead.

Right: No 40.129, also fitted with outside box headcodes and dual brakes, arrives at Kings Cross on the afternoon of 17 August 1974 with the 1A23 09.28 summer Saturdays only dated service from Scarborough. Although not programmed to do so, it was certainly not uncommon to see London Midland Region based members of the class in this London terminus. In recent years, however, any representatives of the class have become progressively more rare here, and are usually only seen on specials and when there are failures.

63

Left: One of a number of Class 40s allocated to Gateshead depot on the Eastern Region, No 40.085 rumbles through Bingley in Yorkshire with the 7E84 07.30 SX Mandatory freight from Carlisle to Tinsley Yard on 5 August 1976. / *S. Varley*

Below: The only Longsight Manchester-based Class 40, fitted with outside box headcodes, No 40.135, stands inside Crewe traction maintenance depot with two of the latter depot's large allocation of Class 47s on the evening of 22 February 1977. The locomotive had undergone a daily examination on number one road, and was awaiting transfer to the nearby holding sidings and eventual allocation to a freight or parcels train.

Right: Whilst based at Healey Mills, (ie before its transfer to Gateshead motive power depot), No 40.152 accelerates away north through Doncaster station with the 6S40 14.55 company grain freight from Belmont Down Yard to Burghead, between Aberdeen and Inverness, on 7 May 1974. The locomotive is, in fact, carrying a slightly incorrect headcode.

Below right: Springs Branch based dual braked Class 40 No 40.172 ascends the Liverpool independent line at Crewe on 18 October 1977. The locomotive is at the head of the 6V93 00.50 MX air braked network service from Mossend to Severn Tunnel Junction, which was introduced on 4 October 1977.

Above: Crewe traction maintenance depot has an allocation of only one class of Type 4 locomotive namely the 47s. This, of course, does not prevent the staff carrying out maintenance on other depots' traction. On 17 February 1978 Nos 40.177 and 40.172, (both allocated to Springs Branch Wigan), were present. The former was undergoing a battery charge whilst the latter was having an 'A' examination. Both locomotives are fitted with dual, air and vacuum, brakes but have had their steam generators isolated.

Left: Although no Class 40s are actually allocated to East Anglian depots they are seen on occasion in the area, particularly on air brake network freights. Here, No 40.068 hauls a Bathgate to Parkeston air brake network freight up Belstead Bank near Ipswich on the Great Eastern on 21 August 1978. / *G. R. Mortimer*

Class 44

Right: One of only three Class 44s still in active service, (they are all based at Toton near Nottingham on the London Midland Region). No 44.004 makes a very rare visit on to Western Region metals. It is seen on 26 August 1976 passing through Hatherley between Cheltenham and Gloucester with the 8V52 13.10 mixed freight from Toton to Westbury. After disposing of the train at Gloucester New Yard the locomotive returned to its home maintenance depot with its Toton train crew and Saltley conductor.

Below: When built as prototypes for the rest of the 'peaks', namely Classes 45 and 46, all the Class 44s were fitted with disc type headcodes. No 44.009 is, however, the only member to have had these replaced on one end only by an inside four character blind-style headcode after a collision several years ago.

Top: No 44.010 still carrying its nameplate *Tryfan* makes its way light back to Toton traction maintenance depot on 10 April 1974 after working the 7E03 SX Conditional freight from Washwood Heath to Tinsley. The locomotive was finally withdrawn on 26 May 1977, having been put into store unserviceable on 1 February 1976, returned to traffic 8 April 1976, withdrawn from stock 18 September 1976 and reinstated instead of No 44.001 on 30 November 1976.

Above: No 44.004 stands in Heron Close loop on the evening of 26 August 1976 with a mixed freight from the London Midland Region to Westbury whilst another Toton based locomotive No 45.074 approaches at speed with the 1V94 14.43 passenger service from Leeds to Plymouth.
No 45.074 is one of several Toton allocated engines mysteriously to gain numbers at all four ends of the locomotive, contrary to British Rail policy.

Class 45

45 043

THE KING'S OWN
ROYAL BORDER REGIMENT

Top: Before its transfer to Tinsley Sheffield, No 45.021 speeds towards Badgeworth Road Bridge near Churchdown with the southbound 1V88 10.12 Newcastle to Taunton on 11 July 1977. Before being transferred to Tinsley this locomotive, together with several of its sister engines in the same class, had spent its entire life at Leeds Holbeck motive power depot.

Above: Close up of Class 45/0 No 45.043 cab side details, showing the number specification panel and nameplate: *The King's Own Royal Border Regiment.*

Top: Taking its first service after being freshly out-shopped from Derby Works after undergoing a general overhaul, No 45.027 is in immaculate condition when seen standing in Bristol Temple Meads whilst hauling the 1V62 07.04 Derby to Plymouth service on 3 October 1975. Unfortunately the locomotive developed faults on its return journey and had to return to works for rectification.

Above: Whilst undergoing its last major overhaul in main works, No 45.043 had its outside head codes removed and sealed beam headlights fitted instead. It is seen some weeks later pausing in Cheltenham Spa station whilst in charge of the 1V94 14.43 Leeds City to Plymouth service on 13 May 1976.

Top: Before departing from St Pancras station on Saturday 16 March 1974 the driver of Peak Class 45/0 No 122 gives a group of train spotters a quick run through of his cab controls whilst another youngster looks on. This shot of the 1D52 service to Nottingham was taken whilst the locomotive was still fitted with only vacuum brakes, ie before it entered Derby Works for a general overhaul to receive the dual brake modification and to be renumbered 45.070.

Above: Fitted with a unique form of headcode lights, No 45.071 passes Alstone sidings (whilst allocated to Leeds Holbeck MPD), on its way to Cheltenham Spa station on 17 August 1976 with the 1V93 09.55 service from Edinburgh to Plymouth. The train engine was involved in a crash at Bridgwater on the Western Region in the autumn of 1974 whilst working a Derby to Exeter freight, and so was fitted with the prototype headcode during its repair.

Left: Close up of cab side and nose details of Class 45/1 No 45.130 stabled on Crewe motive power depot on 18 January 1978.

Above: The driver of Class 45/1 No 45.110 awaits the right away at Leicester whilst working the 1C41 10.50 Nottingham to St Pancras service on 4 June 1976.

Right: No 45.120 rumbles through Broadbottom station on the Manchester Sheffield Wath DC overhead electrified line on Saturday 27 May 1978 with the 1Z33 07.00 St Pancras to Dinting and York enthusiasts special. The train should have been hauled by two of the Class 76 dc electrics which normally work only freight over the route from Godley to Rotherwood. Because the wires were down near Woodhead Tunnel the Class 45/1 was not replaced until the special arrived at Pennistone station.

Above: No 45.123 *The Lancashire Regiment,* fitted with dual brakes and electric train heating equipment, runs into Bristol Temple Meads station on Sunday 21 July 1974 with a Nottingham to Taunton working. The locomotive is one of only nine in the subdivision to carry a nameplate. They all depict famous regiments.

Left: The entire Class 45/1 subdivision is allocated to Toton MPD, and here one of them No 45.129 winds its way past Leicester North signalbox into the station with the 1M15 09.16 service from Leeds City to St Pancras on 4 June 1976. No 45.129 only took the train over at Nottingham Midland where the service reverses and the inward locomotive goes to the near-by stabling point for fuel.

Top right: Shortly before entering Derby Works to undergo a general overhaul and electric train heat conversion, 'Peak' Class 45/0 No 92 is seen coming to a halt in Lansdown loop near Cheltenham on 24 January 1974 with the 8V59 conditional Toton to Severn Tunnel freight. After undergoing the modification the locomotive became a Class 45/1 No 45.138.

Right: No 45.147 leaves Derby station on Sunday 18 June 1978 with the 1M47 14.55 Sheffield to St Pancras service.

Class 46

Top left: The entire series of 'Peak' Type 4 Class 46 locomotives is now allocated to either Plymouth Laira on the Western Region or Gateshead Newcastle on the Eastern. Here one of the former's allocation, No 46.001, stands in Derby station with the Sunday only 1V87 16.12 service to Plymouth.

Above: On a somewhat mundane duty for a Type 4 locomotive, Class 46 No 46.014 is seen in Temple Meads parcels platform with a train of engineer's department open wagons on 11 November 1976.

Left: Class 46 No 46.023 flashes across Brockhampton level crossing with the mid-afternoon 1V86 'Devonian' from Leeds to Paignton on 24 May 1974. Unfortunately three Western Region members of the class, Nos 46.003, 46.005 and 46.024, have been withdrawn because major parts need replacing due to collision damage sustained in traffic.

77

Top: Gateshead based Class 46 No 46.029 hurries through Peterborough station on the afternoon of 1 June 1976 with the 6S45 12.25 Northfleet to Uddington company air braked block Blue Circle cement freight. All remaining 53 members of the class are now fitted with dual brakes and retain steam generators for carriage heating purposes.

Above: Shortly before being transferred from Cardiff Canton to Gateshead, Class 46 No 46.049, fitted with sealed beam headlights after a recent works general overhaul, runs into Cheltenham Spa station with the 8E63 04.55 SX conditional Radyr to Scunthorpe coal freight on 28 April 1976.

Class 47

Above: The Class 47/0 subdivision, by definition means that all the Brush Type 4s in it are fitted with dual brakes and an operative steam generator. As stated in the introduction this no longer applies in every case. One engine that does follow the general rule is No 47.001, allocated to Bristol Bath Road. It is seen here recessed at Gresty Lane near Crewe on the evening of 21 March 1978 with the 6V78 17.38 (TTho) Middlewich to Brighton Ferry company block air-braked salt freight.

Left: Although only two Stratford based Class 47/0s had Union Jacks painted on their sides in connection with the Queen's Silver Jubilee in 1977 most of the depot's remaining steam generator fitted specimens had their roofs and buffers painted silver to brighten up their appearance. One such locomotive, No 47.006, was still in possession of its silver roof when seen working 1N27 11.42 Norwich to London Liverpool Street up Belstead bank on the Great Eastern Main line on 21 August 1978.
/ *G. R. Mortimer*

THE NATIONAL TRUST FOR SCOTLAND

RAILWAY VIADUCT

THIS 510' LONG VIADUCT, WHICH WAS DESIGNED FOR THE INVERNESS AND PERTH JUNCTION RAILWAY (THE HIGHLAND RAILWAY COMPANY FROM 1865) BY JOSEPH MITCHELL WAS COMPLETED IN 1863 AT A COST OF £5,730. THE TEN MASONRY ARCHES ARE EACH 35' SPAN AND THE EXTREME HEIGHT TO THE PARAPET WALL IS 54'.

Top left: Close up of two Class 47 nameplates: No 47.080 *Titan* and No 47.088 *Samson.*

Below: A Western Region Class 47/0 No 47.020 is seen on unusual metals as it speeds southwards through Arbroath with the 1C65 12.35 Aberdeen to Edinburgh on 28 July 1978. No 47.020 was one of the first of the class to be allocated to Plymouth Laira, but has recently been transferred back to Bristol Bath Road.

Right: The Perth to Inverness main line must surely travel through some of the most picturesque countryside in the Central Highlands. Here, Eastfield based Class 47/0 No 47.045 traverses the viaduct at Killiecrankie on the single line between Pitlochry to the south and Blair Atholl to the north, with the 1N32 13.10 Glasgow Queen Street to Inverness on 1 August 1978.

Left: After being involved in a mishap at Stoke Gifford and sustaining severe superficial accident damage, No 47.063 is seen in the process of being rerailed on 4 January 1977. The derailment occurred whilst the locomotive was shunting the wagons for the 23.12 stone train to Appleford out of the yard.

Above: As mentioned earlier in connection with the Queen's Silver Jubilee Celebrations in 1977, the staff at Stratford diesel depot in East London painted Union Jacks on the sides of two of their Brush Class 47/0s. Above No 47.163 leaves Manningtree on the evening of 22 June whilst below, the other, No 47.164, slows in readiness to stop at Ipswich station on 11 August. Unfortunately both have now lost their modified liveries, the former after being involved in a collision with No 83.004 whilst working a freightliner in the Willesden area and undergoing extensive repair in Crewe Works although the latter had its Union Jack painted out before being transferred to York and eventually to Healey Mills. / *G. R. Mortimer*

Left: Shortly after passing Shireoaks East Junction signalbox, Tinsley based No 47.175 makes its way east with the 6E81 11.23 conditional merry-go-round freight from Avenue sidings near Clay Cross Junction to Immingham coal concentration depot.

Below: Crewe based Class 47/0 No 47.204 with its steam generator isolated stands in Sheffield Midland station after arriving with and running round the stock forming the 1M51 09.45 Manchester Piccadilly to St Pancras on Sunday 18 September 1975. This is the only diesel hauled daytime service between the two cities.

Right: Sporting a new pair of lime green buffers, Crewe based Class 47/3 No 47.337 fitted with slow speed running control, ascends the Liverpool independent line at Crewe on 3 November 1977 with the 6V93 00.55 MX Mossend to Severn Tunnel Junction air-braked network service.

Below right: No 47.350 is lifted clear of its bogies whilst undergoing an examination in Crewe diesel depot, which happens to be the locomotive's home maintenance depot, on the evening of 21 February 1977. The locomotive is one of 81 members of the Class 47/3 subdivision, none of which has ever been fitted with any form of carriage heating equipment.

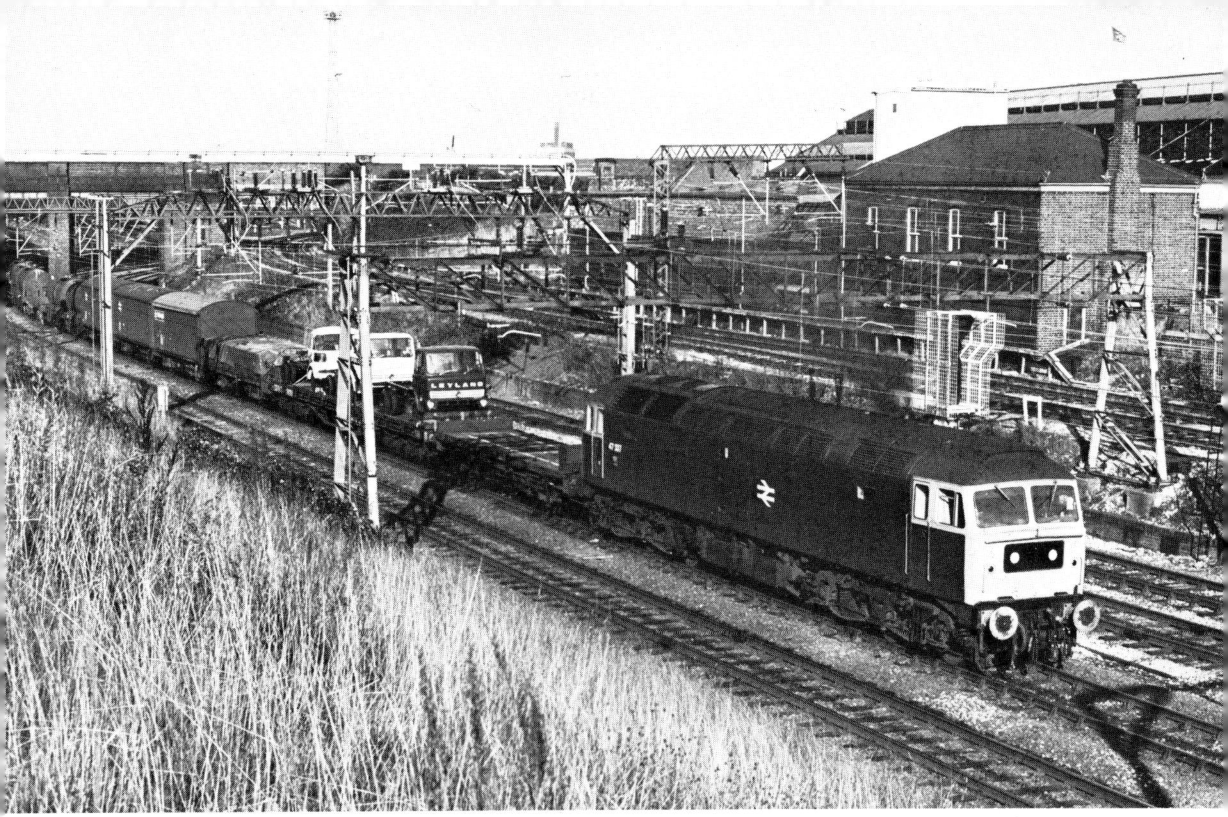
LEYLAND

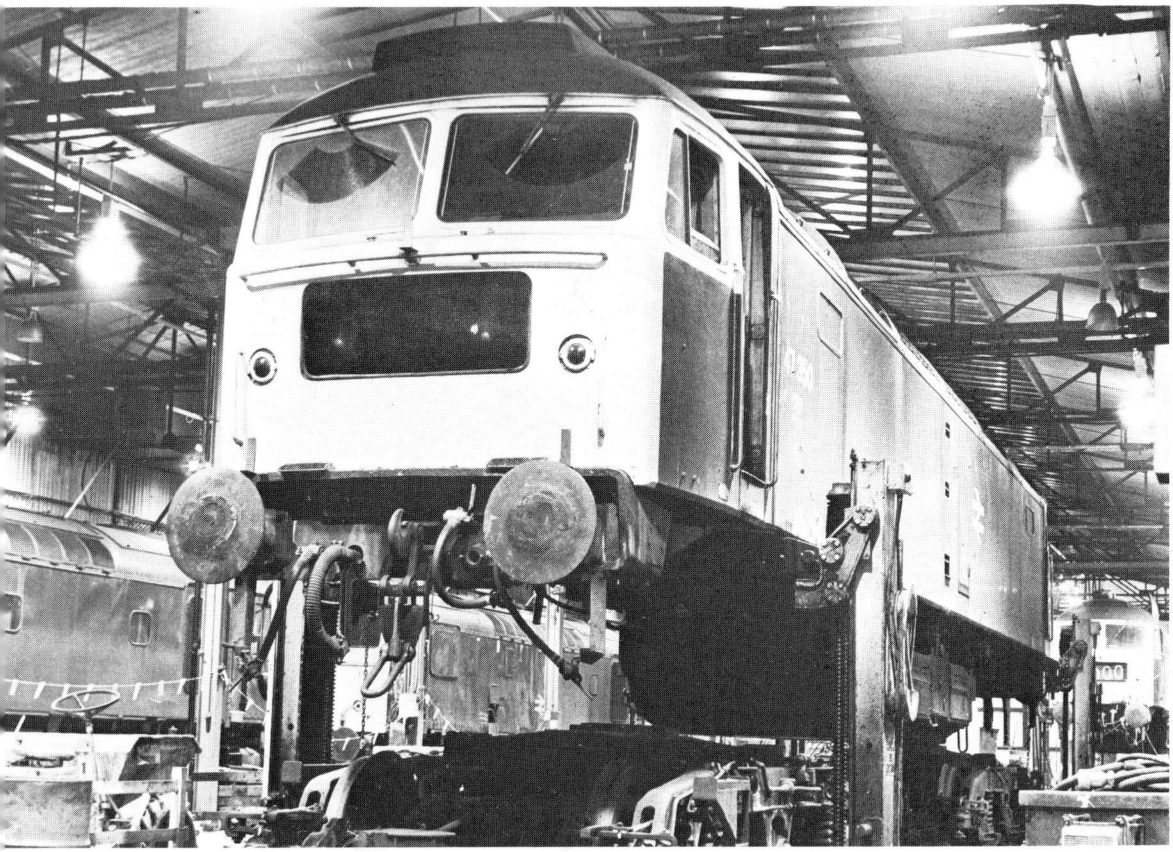

Left: Some distance from home, Bescot based Class 47/3 No 47.341 rumbles into Blair Atholl with the 7D14 13.22 Inverness Yard to Mossend freight on 26 July 1978. The Inverness train crew usually work the freight as far as Ballinluig before changing cabs with the Perth men on the northbound 'Clansman' from Euston.

Below: One of only 13 Class 47s allocated to Thornaby motive power depot near Middlesbrough No 47.361 is fitted with slow speed running control and dual brakes. It is captured crossing King Edward Bridge Junction shortly after passing Gateshead depot, with the 6K62 13.46 SX Jarrow to Tees Port conditional company oil train on 6 April 1977.

Right: A general Sunday shot of Knottingley depot. The scene depicts nine of the depot's allocation of 17 Class 47s all fitted with slow speed running control and which are utilised extensively on merry-go-round services from local Yorkshire collieries to Eggborough and Ferrybridge power stations. The nine Brush Type 4s 'on shed' are Nos 47.179/292/301/2/4/ 19/ 71 /75 and 76, whilst No 08.305 can be seen stabled to the right before being transferred to Healey Mills. / *M. J. Wixey*

Below right: Class 47/4 No 47.406, fitted with both electric train heating and an operative steam generator, stands in Kings Cross on 22 February 1975 after arriving with 1A06 06.30 from Newcastle.

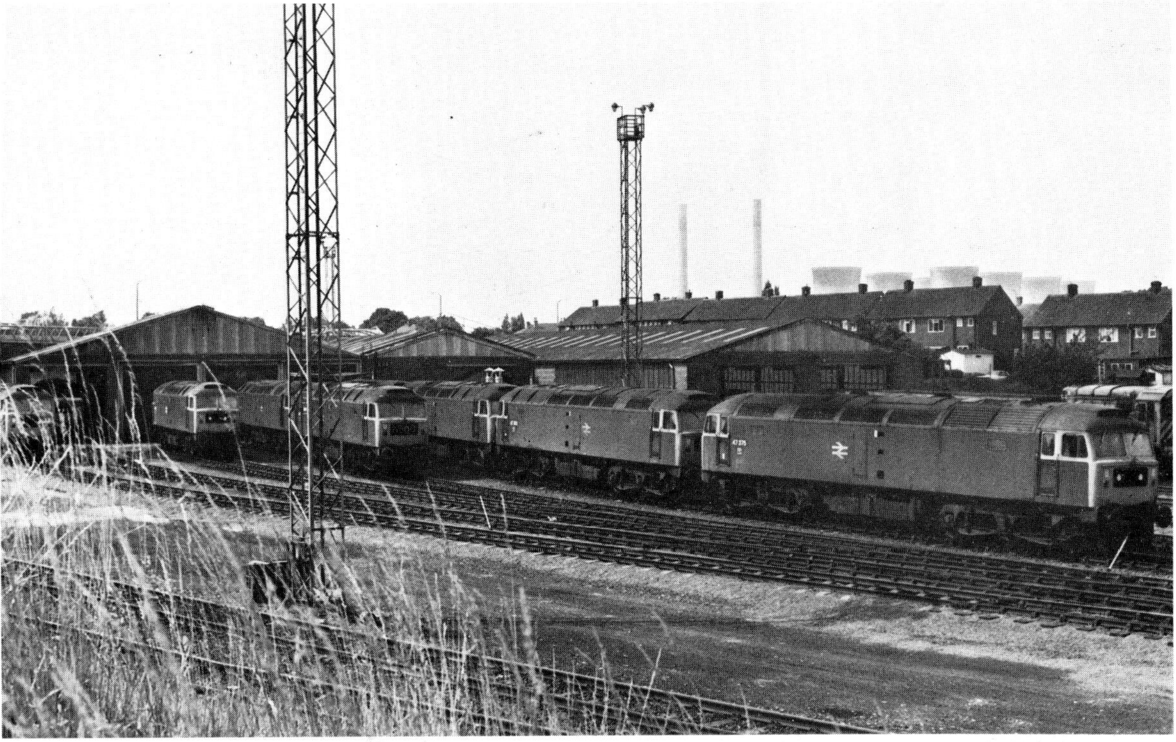

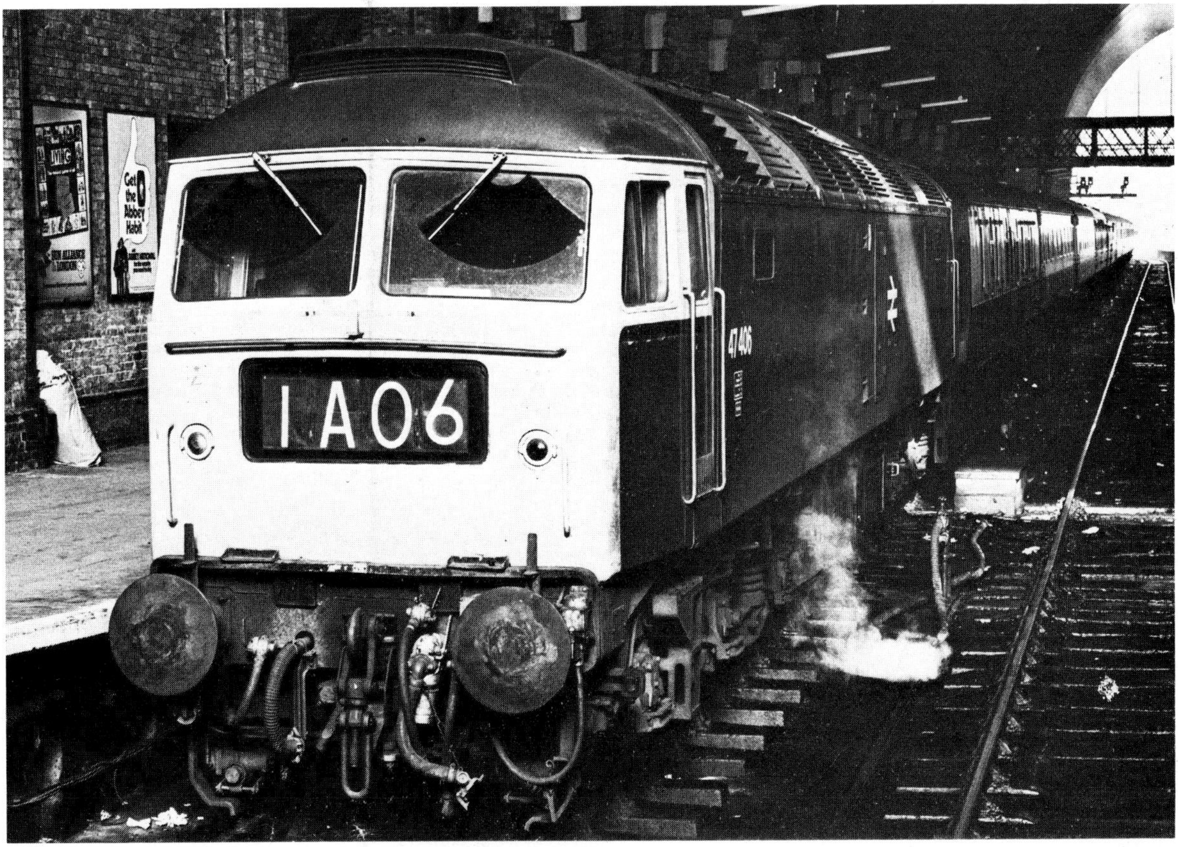
1A06
47 406
Get the Abbey Habit

Above: Two Class 47s prepare to meet under the signal gantry to the west of Chester station on 3 June 1978. To the right, No 47.104 runs in with the 1Z79 06.20 'Mystery Excursion' from Swansea to Blackpool, whilst No 47.454 leaves with the 1D25 09.28 summer-dated Saturday only Birmingham to Llandudno service.

Right: Eastern Region, dual heat fitted, Class 47/4 No 47.425, allocated to Gateshead motive power depot, speeds north across the Hermitage viaduct near Dunkeld with the 1S59 09.36 'Clansman' from Euston to Inverness on 1 August 1978.

Top right: Whilst allocated to Stratford MPD in east London earlier this year, a number of dual heated Brush Type 4 Class 47/4s were spruced up and had their roofs and buffers painted silver and buffer beams painted bright red. One such locomotive to receive this treatment was No 47.458, now allocated to York. It is seen in Edinburgh Waverley station shunting the stock for the 1A38 14.45 to Aberdeen on 27 July 1978. It later worked this train.

Far right: Unusual motive power in the shape of Class 47/4 No 47.522, allocated to Gateshead, Newcastle-upon-Tyne, heads the down 'Day Continental' from Liverpool Street to Parkeston Quay through Mistley on 11 June 1978. / G. R. Mortimer

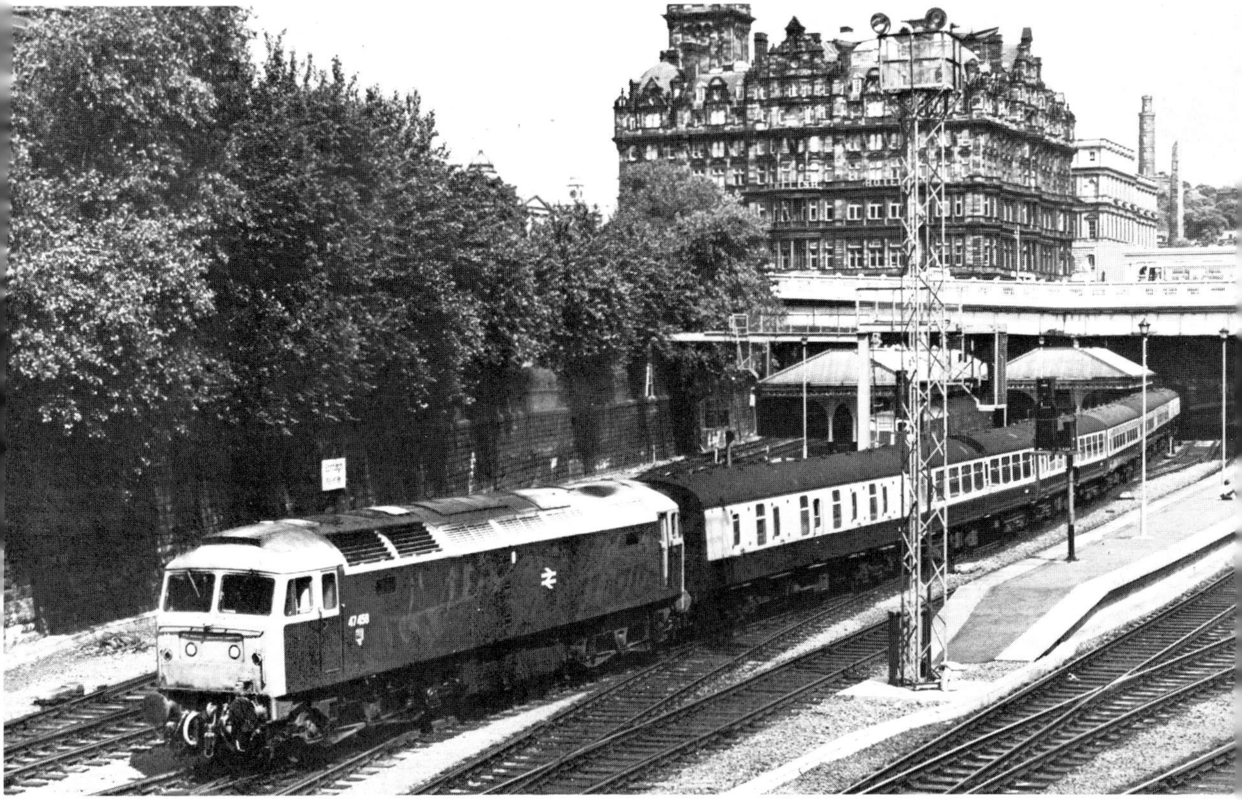

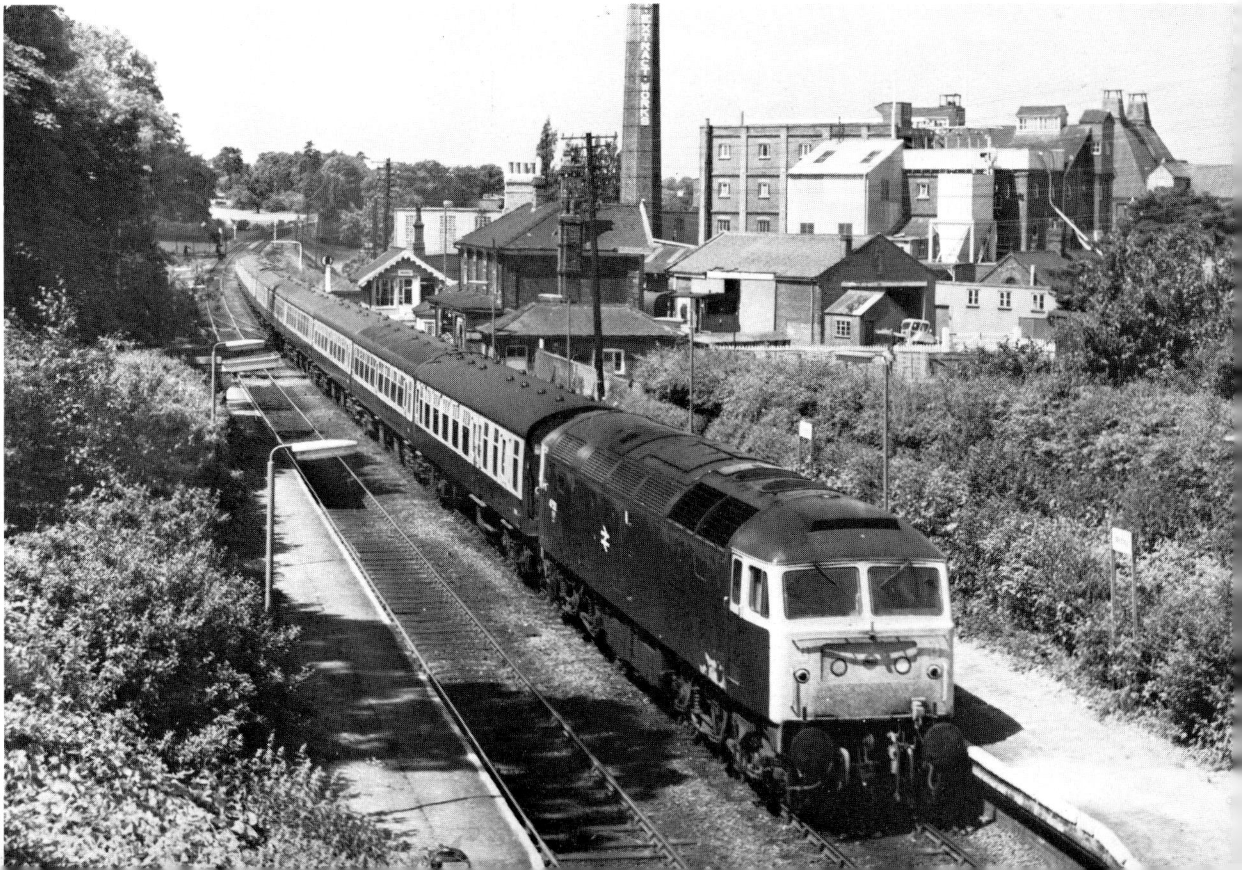

Right: For maintenance purposes (especially on Sundays) the power has to be turned off along short sections of the electrified network. On such occasions diesels are required to haul the dead electrics over such stretches of line. Because of this Crewe diesel depot has possibly one of the largest allocations of Brush Class 47/4s, because they are the engines most used for this purpose. It is not only unusual, therefore, but also rather surprising to see this Bescot based Brush 4 No 47.482 hauling No 86.207 on just such a train through Crewe itself on 5 March 1978.

Below: Before being fitted with electric train heating equipment and renumbered 47.554, Brush Type 4 No 1957 emerges from underneath Gloucester Road Bridge Cheltenham on 13 June 1974 with the 1M85 07.40 Penzance to Liverpool service. The locomotive was originally to have been renumbered 47.261. However, it never carried the number because it was decided to remove its boiler and consequently convert it to a Class 47/4.

Far right: Study of Class 47/4 No 47.547 cab front details in close-up.

Class 50

Right: A study of the cab front details on the 50.003 in close up. The locomotive is one of only two to be fitted with sealed beam headcode lights whilst undergoing general overhaul in Crewe works. The main works maintenance of the entire class is now done by Doncaster on the Eastern Region.

Below: Three Class 50s are seen here standing on Bath Road depot. They are Nos 50.016/28 and 40. The entire class is fitted with snow plough brackets, slow speed running control and only electric train heating equipment. They are also fitted for operation in multiple with other locomotives having similar 'Orange Square' classified equipment.

Far right: Nos 50.008 and 50.044 stand in Paddington station awaiting departure to Bristol and Plymouth respectively on 24 April 1976. It is interesting to note that the headcodes of the engines portray their numbers. / *M. J. Wixey*

Below right: On 13 April 1975, No 50.019 is seen slowing to take the east chord from Hawkeridge to Heywood Road junction having been diverted because of engineering work via Bathampton, Bradford and Hawkeridge. Although the train was officially the 1A22 11.15 Bristol to Paddington service, it had had to be retimed to start at 11.45. / *G. R. Hounsell*

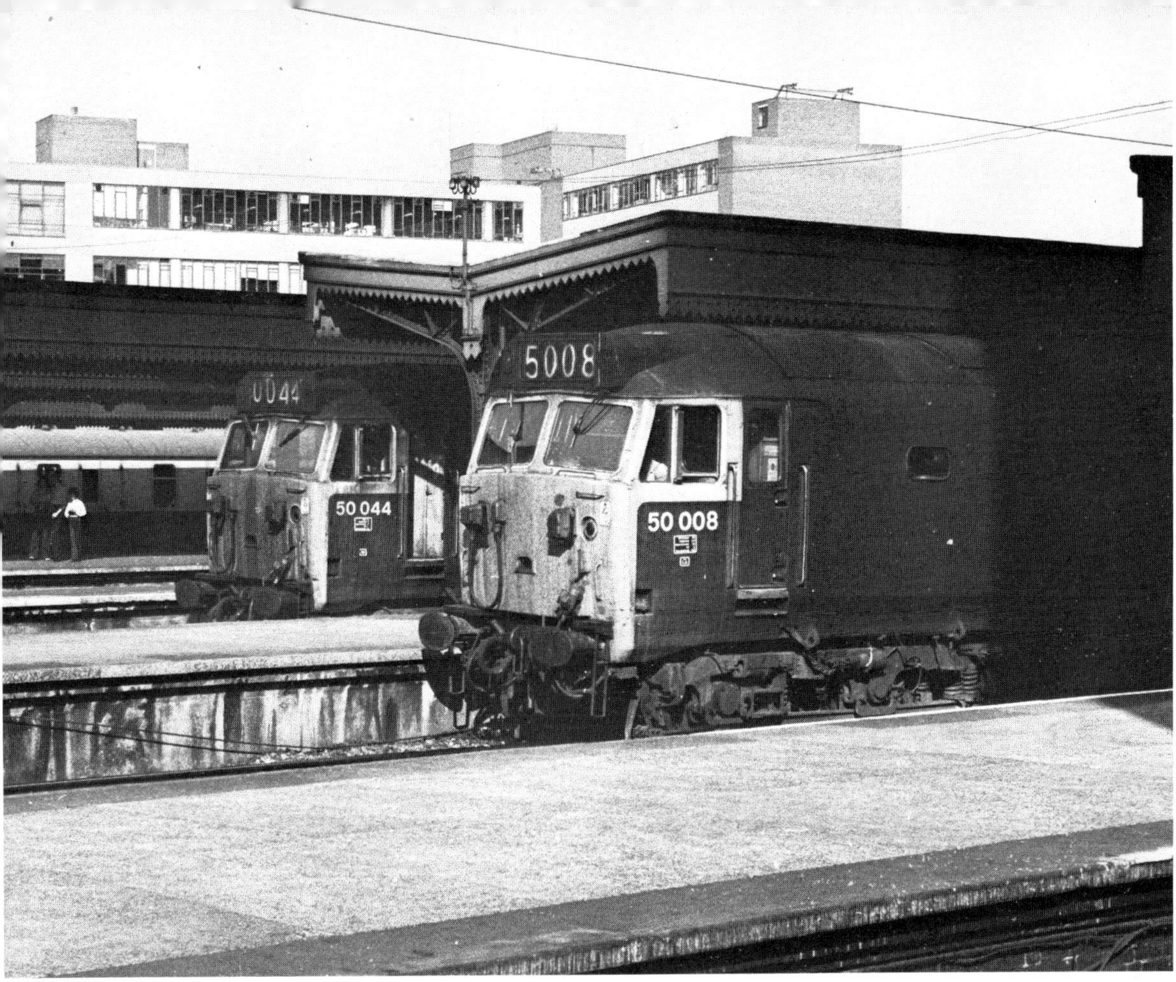
5008
0044
50 044
50 008

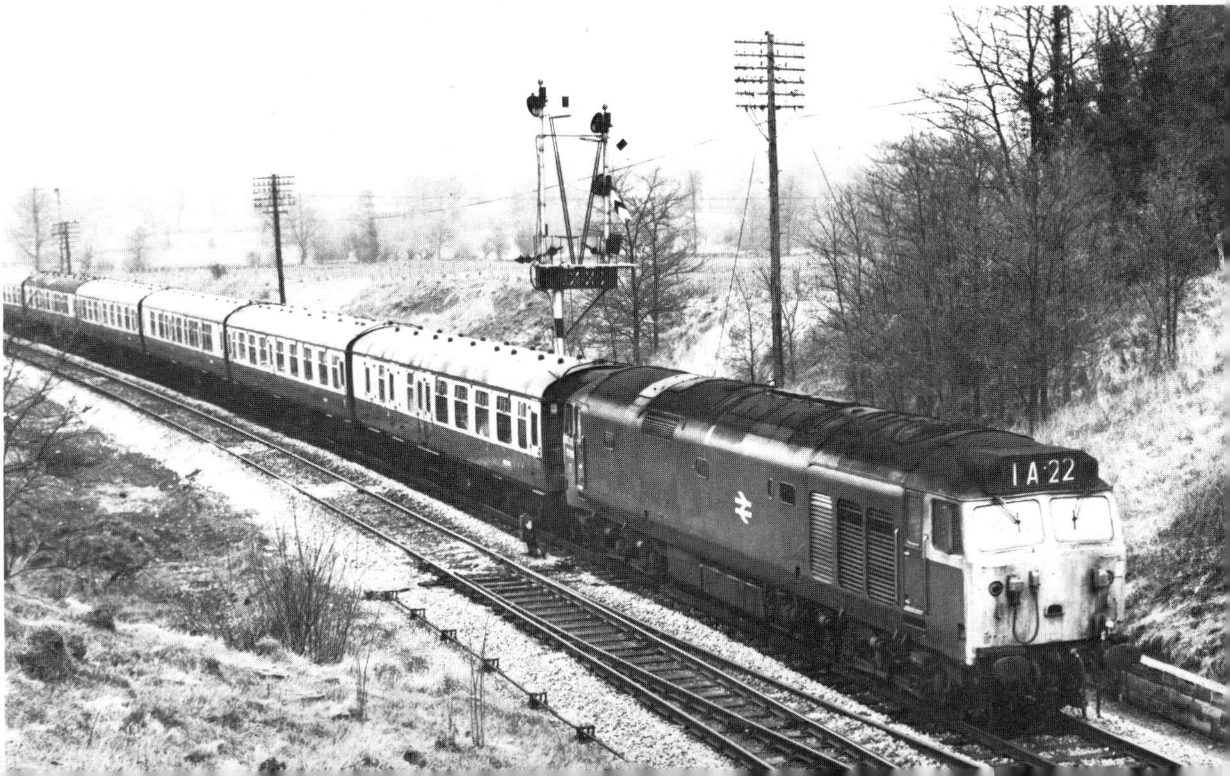
1A22

50 032

Bristol BR	AB-VB	Class	50
	Weight tons		117
	Brake force tons		59
	RA		6
	Max speed·mph		100

Left: Close up of a depot renumbered Class 50 No 50.032 cab side details showing the depot allocation sticker and specification panel.

Below: At the beginning of their lives in 1967/68, the Class 50s were still owned by their makers and only leased to British Rail. These close ups are of the 'on hire' plaque and makers plate of Nos 50.032 and 50.047 repectively.

Right: No 50033 powers through Saltford to the West of Bath Spa on 19 August 1976 with the 1A02 13.30 service from Bristol to Paddington.

THIS LOCOMOTIVE IS THE PROPERTY OF ENGLISH ELECTRIC LEASINGS LIMITED

THE ENGLISH ELECTRIC Co. LTD.
VULCAN WORKS,
NEWTON-LE-WILLOWS, ENGLAND.
No 3816/D1187 1968.

Top: No 50.001 was once allocated to Old Oak Common with four other Class 50 locomotives. During this period it was seen on the morning of 15 September 1976, rumbling out of Bristol Temple Meads station with the 1A30 07.57 Weston-super-Mare to Paddington service.

Above: A somewhat unusual sight is a Class 50 on freight. Here No 50.027 takes the curve at Dr Days junction near Bristol with the 6B36 12.30 Avonmouth to Exeter City Basin Texaco company tank train on 5 March 1976.

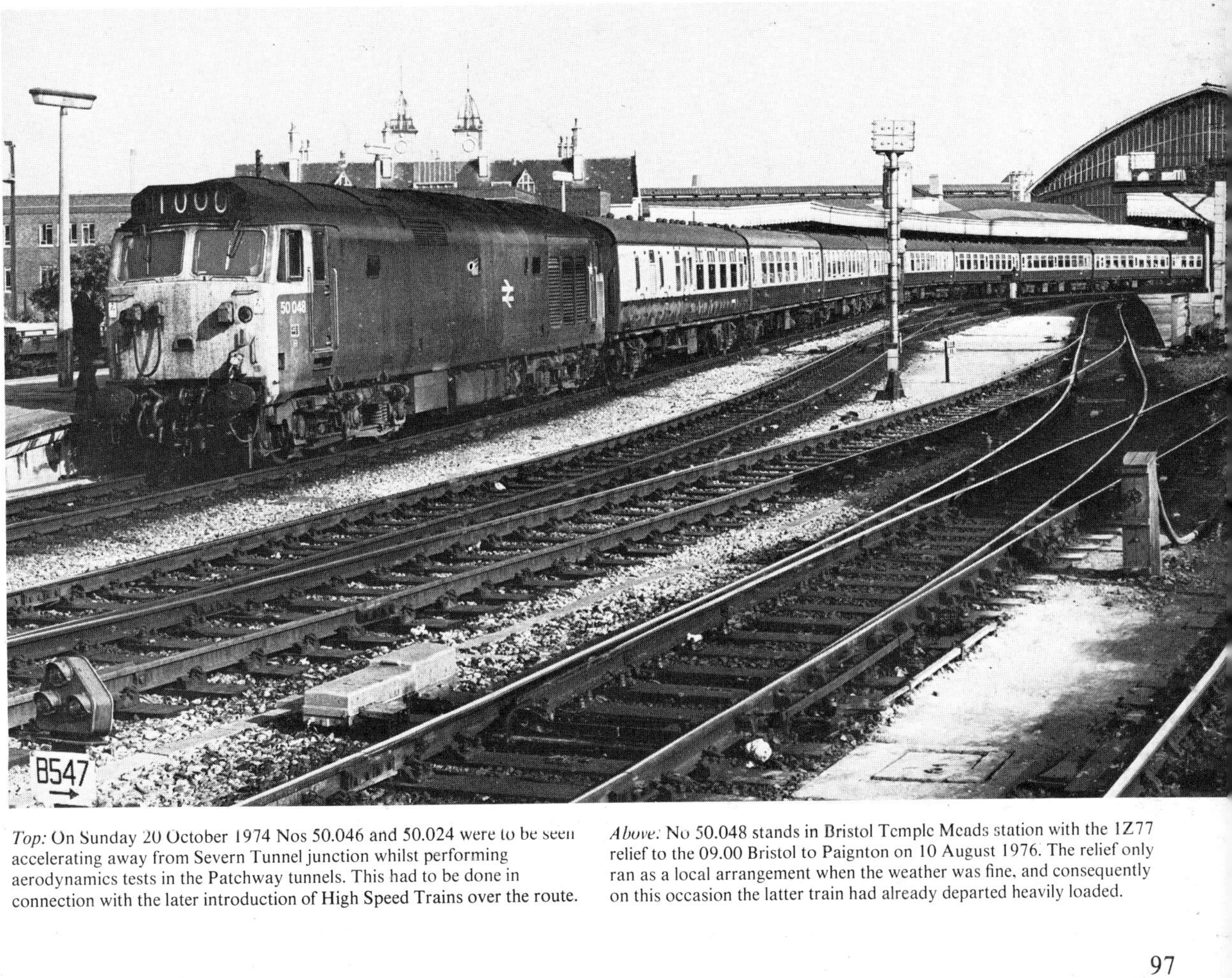

Top: On Sunday 20 October 1974 Nos 50.046 and 50.024 were to be seen accelerating away from Severn Tunnel junction whilst performing aerodynamics tests in the Patchway tunnels. This had to be done in connection with the later introduction of High Speed Trains over the route.

Above: No 50.048 stands in Bristol Temple Meads station with the 1Z77 relief to the 09.00 Bristol to Paignton on 10 August 1976. The relief only ran as a local arrangement when the weather was fine, and consequently on this occasion the latter train had already departed heavily loaded.

97

Class 52

Top left: Class 52 No 1015 *Western Champion* leaves Bristol Temple Meads on Saturday 21 July 1974 with a Paddington to Paignton service.

Left and right: Study of a Class 52 nameplate and numberplate, both in close up.

Above: No 1021 *Western Cavalier* snakes its way round Westerleigh curve after leaving the South Wales-Paddington main line. It was hauling the 1E70 14.30 Paignton to York on 21 July 1976, and as can be seen in the photograph, the end of the train had not crossed the junction at this point in time. Just over three weeks after the shot was taken, the locomotive was condemned after sustaining considerable accident damage when it collided with an 08 shunter in Plymouth Laira carriage sidings.

LA

1068

AB-VB	Class	52
	Weight tons	108
	Brake force tons	50
	RA	6
	Max speed mph	90

Top: A regular turn of duty for the Class 52s which took them on to LMR metals almost every day right up until their final withdrawal was to haul the clayliner. Here, No 1035, *Western Yeoman*, heads the southbound 6V53 04.27 MX Stoke to St Blazey china clay empties through Cheltenham on 27 November 1973.

Above: Most Class 52s had windscreen wipers hung from the top of the windows, but in the case of No 1045 *Western Viscount*, the drivers assistant side wiper was altered to the bottom and vents were added to the top. These modifications are clearly visible on the locomotive as it heads the 3B01 Worcester-Bristol parcels, through Granleyfield on the evening of 3 June 1974.

Top right: The penultimate Class 52 to undergo a general overhaul in Swindon works, No 1058 *Western Nobleman*, runs into Reading General on 9 April 1974 with the IC68 from Paddington to Swansea.

Right: A storm brews as No 1065 *Western Consort* leaves Bristol Temple Meads station after a crew change on 4 October 1976. It is about to head south with the 6V53 04.27 Stoke yard to St Blazey china clay empties. At the time the photograph was taken, reporting numbers had been discontinued and so most Class 52s carried their own number there instead.

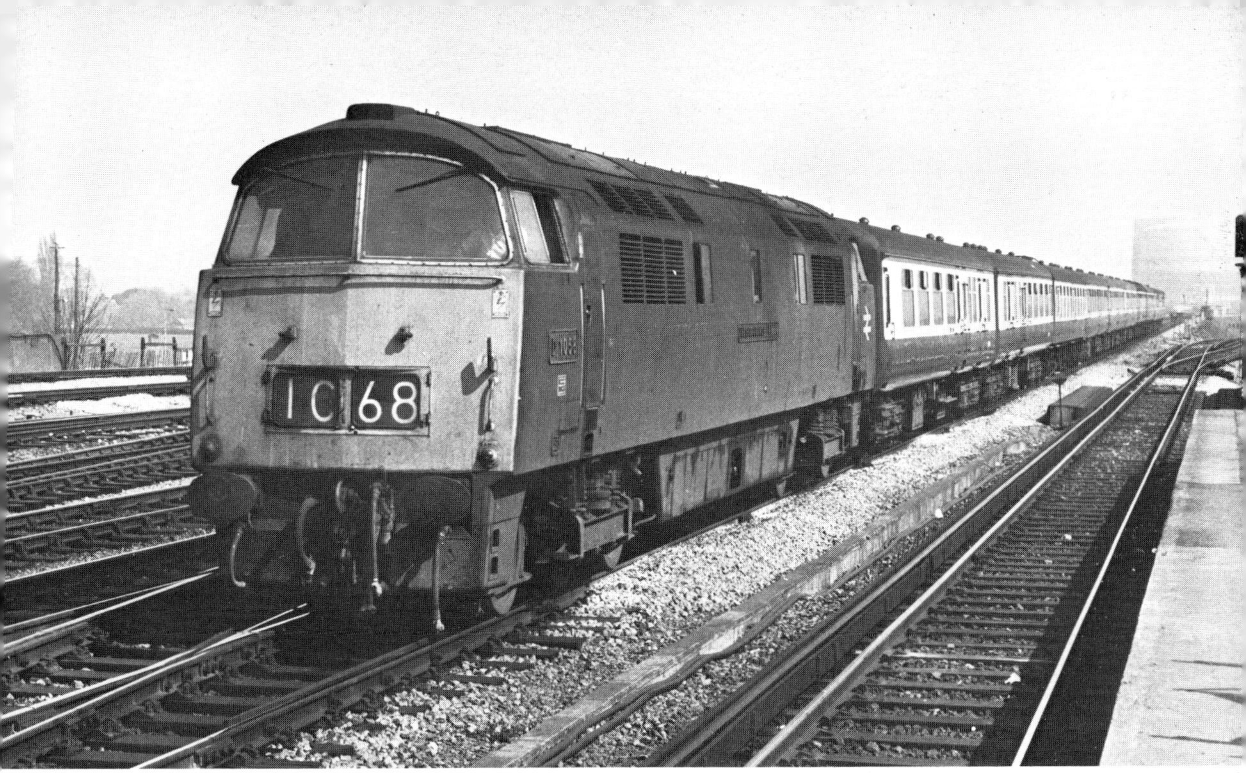
1C68

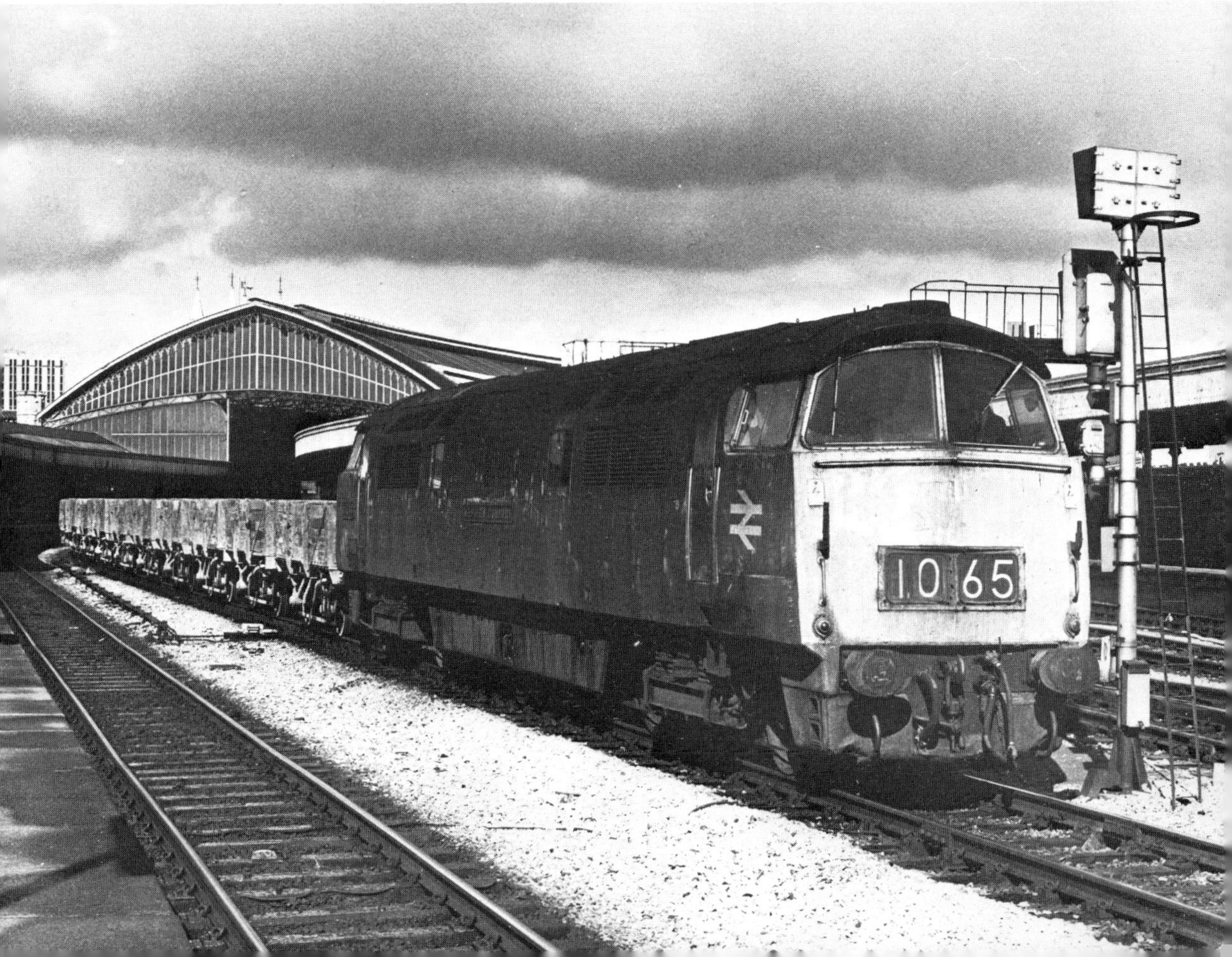
1O65

Below: Only one Class 52 ever gained dot headcodes, apparently because the Eastern Region would not accept it on a special on their metals unless it conformed to their operating requirements. The locomotive No 1023 *Western Fusilier*, now preserved in York Railway Museum, coasts through the Welsh countryside near Pontrilas with the 1Z08 08.20 Western Memorial special from Paddington to Crewe on 29 January 1977.

Class 55

Right: With the coming of the High Speed Trains on the East Coast main line the Class 55s have been relegated to more mundane tasks. Here, Gateshead based No 55.002 *The Kings own Yorkshire Light Infantry*, fitted with the all yellow modified headcode panelling, speeds through Retford Great Northern on 30 May 1978 with the 1A71 12.25 relief from Newcastle to Kings Cross, comprised of a mixture of Mk 1 and early Mk II stock.

Below: 'Deltic' Class 55 No 55.001 *St Paddy*, stands in Doncaster station on 7 April 1974 with the 1E13 12.20 Edinburgh to Kings Cross service. All the Finsbury Park based 'Deltics', of which No 55.001 is one, are named after famous race horses.

Below: 'Deltic' nameplate *Ballymoss* in close up.

Bottom: Study of Class 55 No 55.010 *The King's Own Scottish Borderer*, allocated to Haymarket depot in Edinburgh, after undergoing a general overhaul in Doncaster works. On 7 April 1974 the locomotive was standing in the works yard.

Right: Before the four character headcode system was discontinued Class 55 No 55.002 is again seen, this time running into Kings Cross with the 1A22 13.50 service from Newcastle. Since May 1978 this particular service has been worked by the Eastern Region's newly-acquired Inter-City 125 Class 254 units.

Below right: The appearance of the 'Deltic' Class 55s on Western Region metals is still a rare sight, although they have worked enthusiasts specials and engineers test trains in connection with dipped rail joint experiments on the region. On the first of these specials, No 55.003 *Meld* passes Ebbw junction motive power depot near Newport with the 1Z33 Reading division charter from Paddington to Cardiff on 12 October 1975.

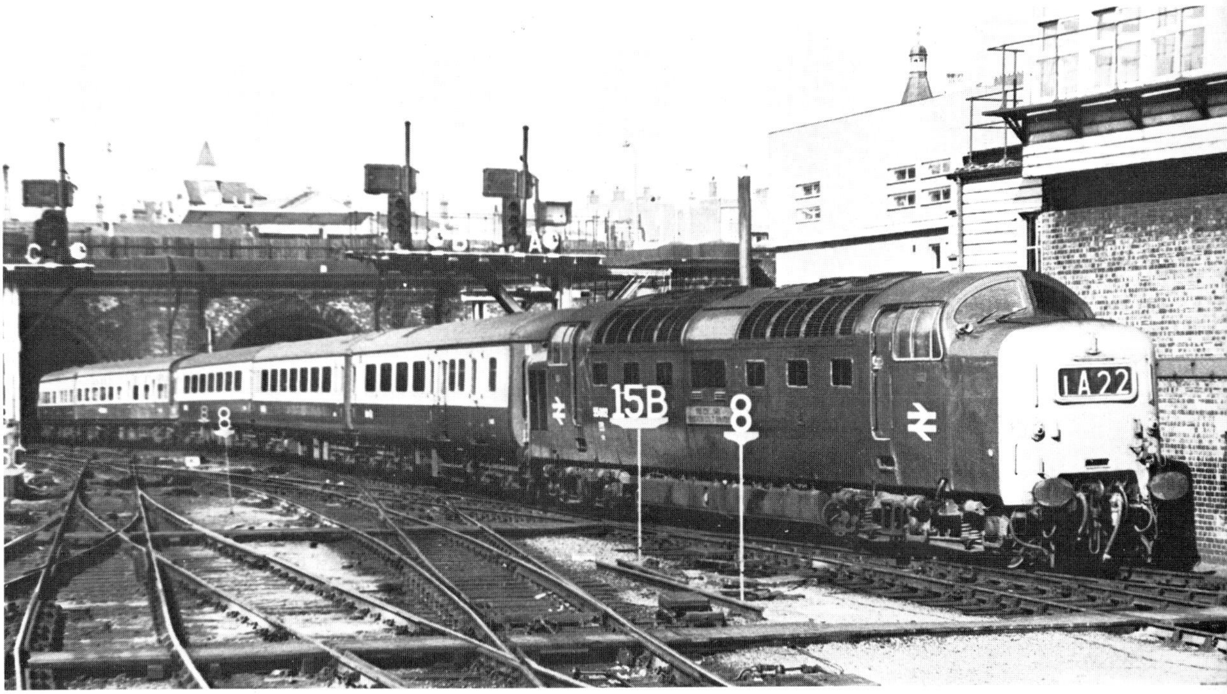

1A22
15B
8
8

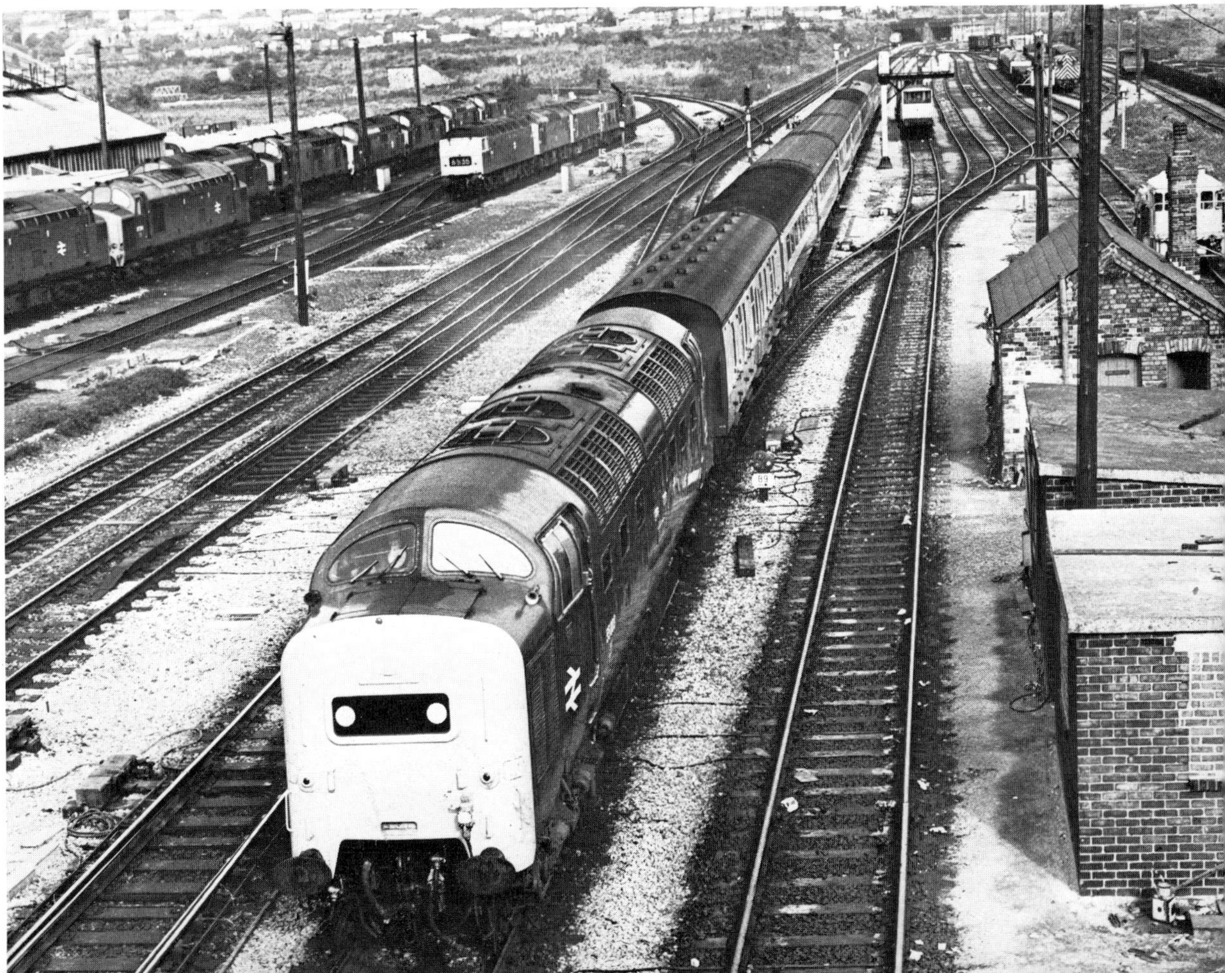

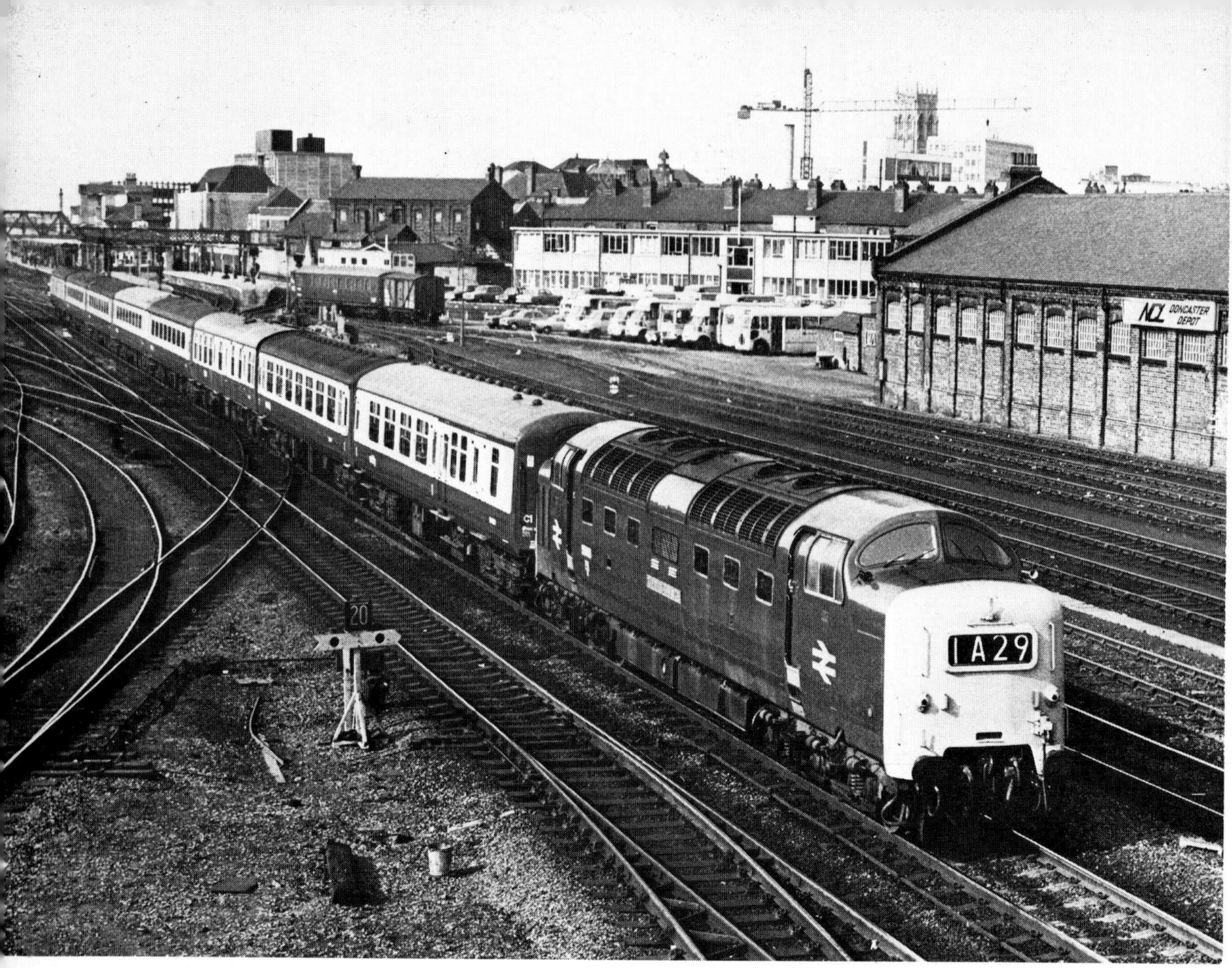
NCL DONCASTER DEPOT
20
1A29

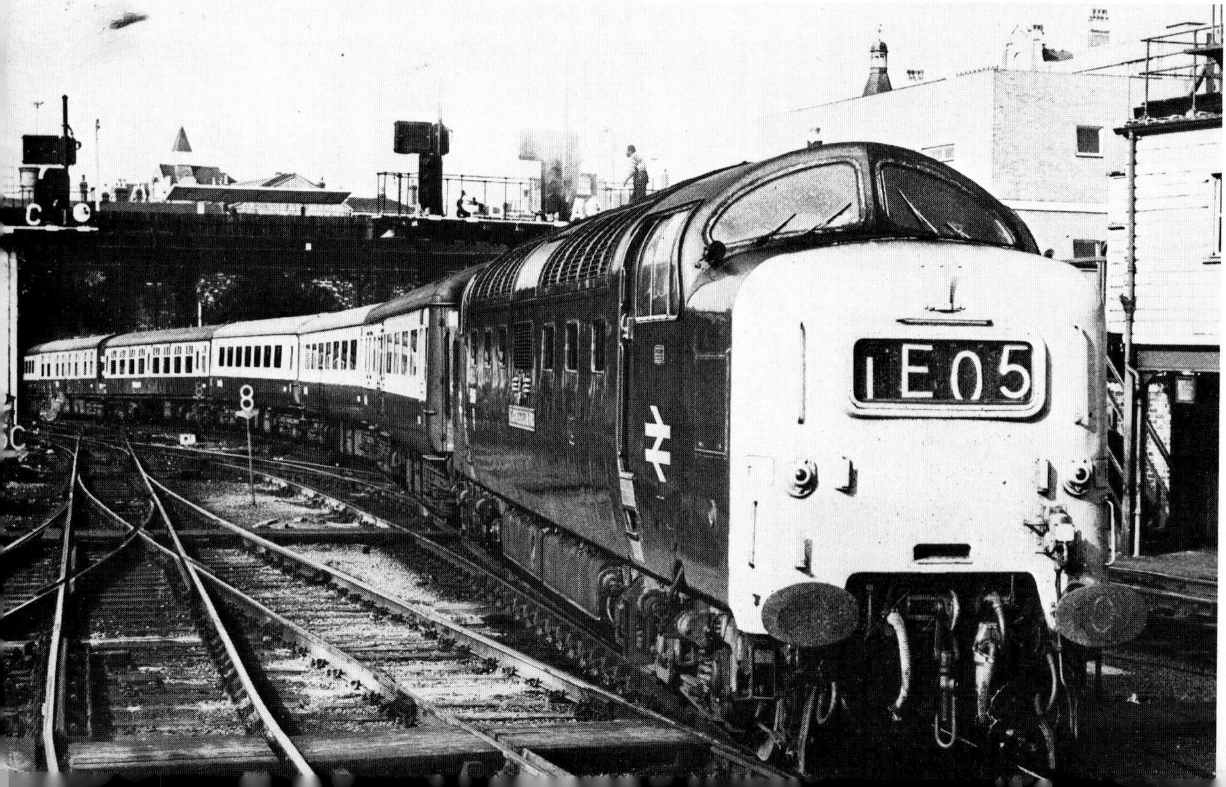
1E05
8

Top left: 'Deltic' No 55.013 *The Black Watch*, speeds through Doncaster on 7 May 1974 with the 1A29 16.20 Leeds to Kings Cross service. All the Haymarket and Gateshead based Class 55s are named after regiments.

Left: On 14 September 1974 the up 'Flying Scotsman', the 1E05 09.55 from Edinburgh, runs into Kings Cross with No 55.016 in charge. This service was the first on the East Coast main line to be worked by Inter-City 125 Class 254 HSTs in May 1978.

Above: No 55.016 *Gordon Highlander* powers southwards towards Retford on 30 May 1978 with the 1E11 09.00 Aberdeen to Kings Cross service.

Right: Class 55 No 55.018 *Ballymoss* makes its way slowly north after leaving Retford Great Northern with the 1L11 14.04 Kings Cross to York on 30 May 1978.

Class 56

Top left: Study of Tinsley allocated, Romanian built Class 56 No 56.014. The first 30 of the class were all built abroad and shipped across the North Sea from Zeebrugge to Harwich, before undergoing commissioning trials on the Eastern Region.

Left: A trio of Romanian built Class 56s are, from left to right, Nos 56.016, 014, and 005 inside the depot building at Shirebrook. The only obvious external differences between the locomotives built in Britain and those built abroad are the window surrounds and the buffer beam ends.

Above: A general shot of Shirebrook motive power depot, showing no less than five Class 56 locomotives amongst the 11 main line locomotives visible. 'On shed' are Nos 31.271/6 20.210/09 37.132/29 56.015/27/09, with Nos 56002 and 016 in the foreground on 30 May 1978.

Right: No 56.017 approaches Shireoaks East Junction at speed with 6F58 12.45 merry-go-round from Seymour Junction to Cottam power station in May 1978. The haze behind the freight of merry-go-round hoppers is caused by the tiny particles of coal dust being blown off the wagons and up into the atmosphere.

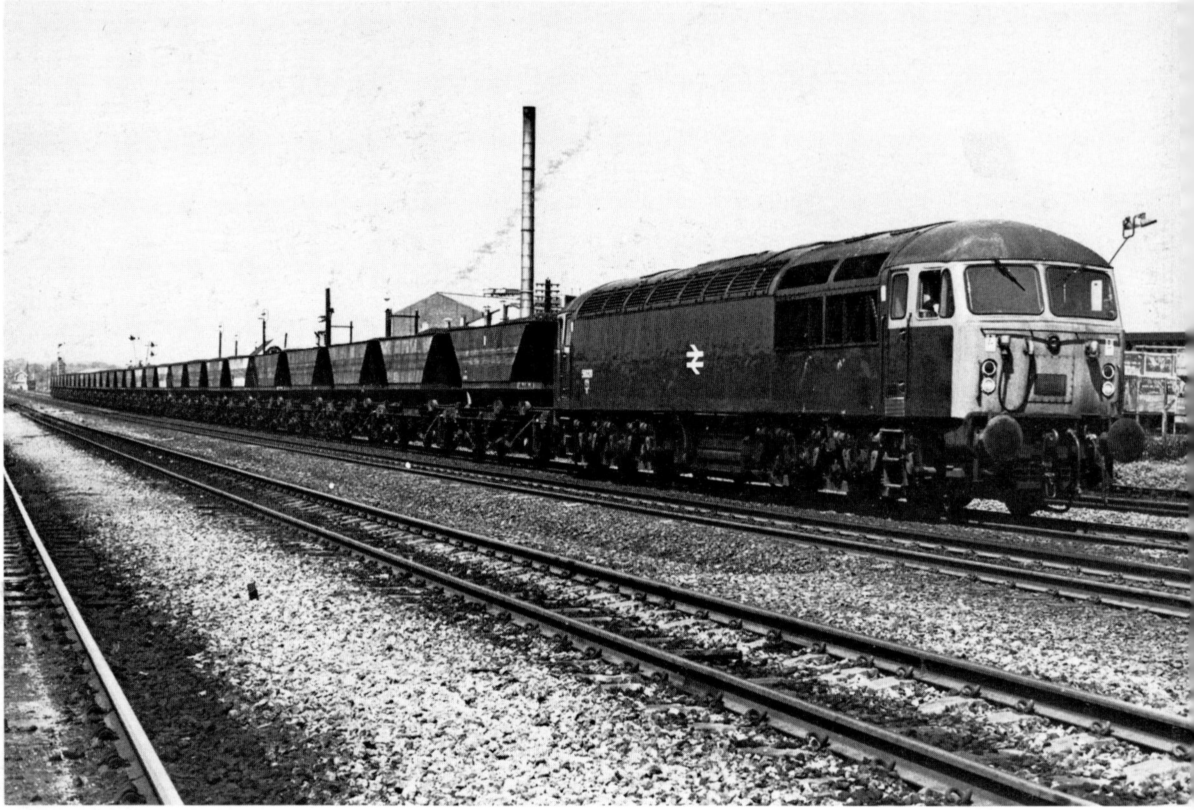

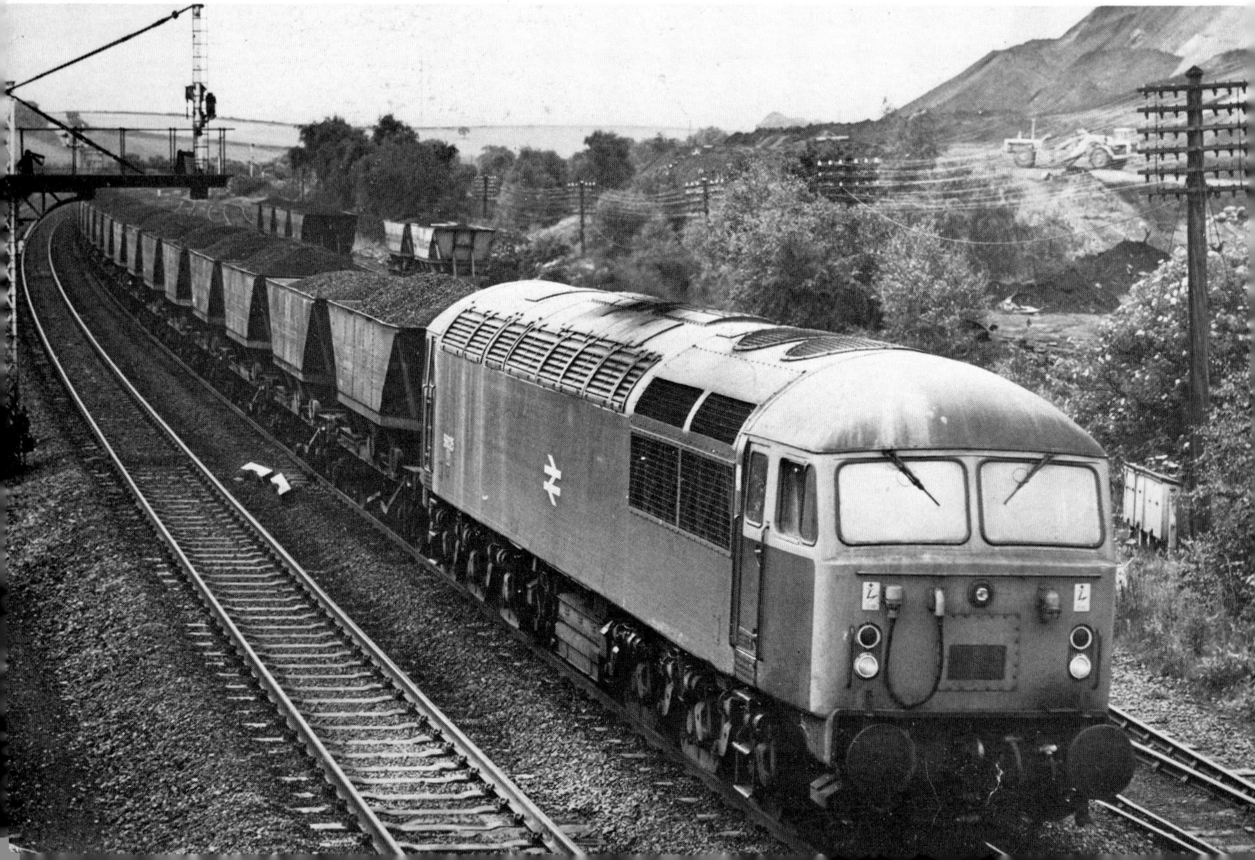

Top left: Fitted with slow speed running control
and with a maximum speed of 80mph,
No 56.020 rumbles through Worksop with the
6F54 mgr freight from Westhorpe Colliery to
Cottam power station. The entire Tinsley based
allocation have undergone extensive bogie
modifications at either Doncaster or Stratford
Works because on commissioning trials the
original bogies had a tendaency to run hot.

Left: Class 56 No 56.025 approaches Renishaw
on the former Midland, Chesterfield to
Rotherham Masborough route with a down
merry-go-round freight from Barrow Hill
/ *L. A. Nixon*

Above: Shortly after passing through Alfreton
and Mansfield Parkway station, No 56.027
accelerates away southwards with a loaded mgr
freight from Avenue sidings to Toton yard,
eventually destined for one of the Midland
power stations. / *L. A. Nixon*

Right: Nearing completion, Class 56 No 56.050
stands alongside the frames of several sister
locomotives whilst under construction in
Doncaster works on 3 September 1978.

Top: The cab fronts but not the roof of No 56.040 had been attached when the locomotive posed with No 56.041 (in an even less finished state) at Doncaster works on 18 September 1977.

Above: Finally, to end the volume, I have decided to use this print of No 56.045 taken on the locomotive's home maintenance depot, Toton. Although it is certainly sad to see so many of British Rail's older classes of locomotive disappear, one cannot but feel that this brand new powerful piece of engineering is not only a tribute to those who designed and built her, but also heralds the arrival of a truly modern railway network.